# AZ

ADVENT

# Surrey Hills

G000269382

■ This new publication covers the Surrey Hills Area of Outstanding Natural Beauty an area of rolling Downland, commons and heathland, all ideal walking country; among the many outstanding features are Box Hill and the Devil's Punch Bowl.

■ Containing Ordnance Survey 'Explorer' maps in a convenient book format with an index to the main features, and showing all footpaths, rights of way and public access land, this is the essential walking companion.

## CONTENTS

Reference / Legend.................2-3
Key to Map Pages...................4-5
Map Pages...........................6-67
Index....................................68-73

Safety & Security...................74-75
Mountain Biking.........................76
QR codes...................................77

## Geographers' A-Z Map Company Limited

Fairfield Road, Borough Green,
Sevenoaks, Kent TN15 8PP
Telephone: 01732 781000 (Enquiries & Trade Sales)
01732 783422 (Retail Sales)
www.az.co.uk
Copyright © Geographers' A-Z Map Company Limited
EDITION 1   2013

Ordnance Survey®

This product includes mapping data licensed from Ordnance Survey® with the permission of the Controller of Her Majesty's Stationery Office.

Mapping contents © Crown copyright and database rights 2012 Ordnance Survey 100017302

# Communications

## ROADS AND PATHS
*Not necessarily rights of way*

 Service Areas

**7** Junction number

M I or A 6(M) — Motorway

A 35 — Dual carriageway

A 30 — Main road

B 3074 — Secondary road

Narrow road with passing places

Road under construction

Road generally more than 4m wide

Road generally less than 4m wide

Other road, drive or track, fenced and unfenced

Gradient: steeper than 20% (1 in 5); 14% (1 in 7) to 20% (1 in 5)

Ferry; Ferry P – passenger only

Path

## RAILWAYS

Multiple track standard gauge

Single track standard gauge

Narrow gauge or Light rapid transit system (LRTS) and station

Road over; road under; level crossing

Cutting; tunnel; embankment

Station, open to passengers; siding

## PUBLIC RIGHTS OF WAY

------------ Footpath ———— Bridleway

++++++ Byway open to all traffic

-+-+-+ Restricted byway (not for use by mechanically propelled vehicles)

Public rights of way shown on this map have been taken from local authority definitive maps and later amendments. Rights of way are liable to change and may not be clearly defined on the ground.
Please check with the relevant local authority for the latest information.

The representation on this map of any other road, track or path is no evidence of the existence of a right of way.

## OTHER PUBLIC ACCESS

• • • Other routes with public access (not normally shown in urban areas)

The exact nature of the rights on these routes and the existence of any restrictions may be checked with the local highway authority. Alignments are based on the best information available.

 National Trail

Long Distance Route and Recreational Route

--------- Permissive footpath

———— Permissive bridleway

Footpaths and bridleways along which landowners have permitted public use but which are not rights of way. The agreement may be withdrawn.

• • • Traffic-free cycle route

1 National cycle network route number – traffic free

**1** National cycle network route number – on road

 Firing and test ranges in the area. Danger! Observe warning notices

Visit www.access.mod.uk for information

## ACCESS LAND

Portrayal of access land on this map is intended as a guide to land which is normally available for access on foot, for example access land created under the Countryside and Rights of Way Act 2000, and land managed by the National Trust, Forestry Commission and Woodland Trust. Access for other activities may also exist. Some restrictions will apply; some land will be excluded from open access rights.
The depiction of rights of access does not imply or express any warranty as to its accuracy or completeness. Observe local signs and follow the Countryside Code.

Visit www.countrysideaccess.gov.uk for up-to-date information

Access land boundary and tint

Access land in woodland area

*i* Access information point

 Access permitted within managed controls for example, local bylaws

Visit www.access.mod.uk for information

# General Information

## BOUNDARIES

— -+- — -+- — National

— · — · — · — County (England)

— — — — Unitary Authority (UA), Metropolitan District (Met Dist), London Borough (LB) or District (Scotland & Wales are solely Unitary Authorities)

· · · · · · · · · · Civil Parish (CP) (England) or Community (C) (Wales)

▬▬▬ ▬▬ National Park boundary

## VEGETATION

*Limits of vegetation are defined by positioning of symbols*

Coniferous trees

Non-coniferous trees

Coppice

Bracken, heath or rough grassland

Marsh, reeds or saltings

 Orchard

Scrub

**3**

## GENERAL FEATURES

| | |
|---|---|
| + | Place of worship |

Current or former place of worship

| | |
|---|---|
| ♦ | with tower |
| ♦ | with spire, minaret or dome |
| ▢ ▢ | Building; important building |
| ▨ | Glasshouse |
| ▲ | Youth hostel |
| ■ | Bunkhouse/camping barn/other hostel |
| ⬣ | Bus or coach station |
| 🗼 🗼 🗼 | Lighthouse; disused lighthouse; beacon |

| | |
|---|---|
| △ ⍭ | Triangulation pillar; mast |
| 🗼 | Windmill, with or without sails |
| ⍭ ⍭ | Wind pump; wind turbine |
| pylon  pole | Electricity transmission line |
| ⟫⟫⟫⟫⟫ | Slopes |

Gravel pit    Sand pit

Other pit or quarry    Landfill site or slag/spoil heap

| | |
|---|---|
| BP/BS | Boundary post/stone |
| CG | Cattle grid |
| CH | Clubhouse |
| FB | Footbridge |
| MP; MS | Milepost; milestone |
| Mon | Monument |
| PO | Post office |
| Pol Sta | Police station |
| Sch | School |
| TH | Town hall |
| NTL | Normal tidal limit |
| ∘W; Spr | Well; spring |

## HEIGHTS AND NATURAL FEATURES

52 ·   Ground survey height

284 ·   Air survey height

Vertical face/cliff

Loose rock    Boulders    Outcrop    Scree

Surface heights are to the nearest metre above mean sea level. Where two heights are shown, the first height is to the base of the triangulation pillar and the second (in brackets) to the highest natural point of the hill.

75
60
50

Contours may be at 5 or 10 metres vertical interval

| | |
|---|---|
| ▢ | Water |
| ▢ | Mud |
| ▢ | Sand; sand & shingle |

## ARCHAEOLOGICAL AND HISTORICAL INFORMATION

| | |
|---|---|
| ⚜ | Site of antiquity |
| ⚔ 1066 | Site of battle (with date) |

| | |
|---|---|
| ⁕ ⁞⁞⁞⁞ | Visible earthwork |
| **VILLA** | Roman |
| 𝕮astle | Non-Roman |

Information provided by English Heritage for England and the Royal Commissions on the Ancient and Historical Monuments for Scotland and Wales

# Selected Tourist and Leisure Information

| | | | | | | | |
|---|---|---|---|---|---|---|---|
| **P** | Parking | ⛺ | Camp site | 🚲 | Cycle hire | 🐟 | Fishing |
| **P&R** | Park & Ride, - all year | 🚐 | Caravan site | ∪ | Horse riding | ☆ | Other tourist feature |
| **P&R** | - seasonal | 🏃 | Recreation leisure sports centre | ☀ | Viewpoint | ✝ | Cathedral/Abbey |
| **𝑖** | Information cen. - all year | ⚑ | Golf course or links | ✕ | Picnic site | 🏛 | Museum |
| **𝑖** | - seasonal | | | | | | |
| **V** | Visitor centre | 🎡 | Theme pleasure park | 👪 | Country park | 🏰 | Castle/fort |
| | | 🚂 | Preserved railway | ❀ | Garden arboretum | 🏛 | Building of historic interest |
| 🌲 | Forestry Commission visitor centre | ☕ | Public house/s | ⛵ | Water activities | HC | Heritage centre |
| PC | Public convenience | ⚒ | Craft centre | ⚓ | Slipway | 🌿 | National Trust |
| ✆ | Telephone - public | ! | Walks/trails | ⛵ | Boat trips | ▦ | English Heritage |
| ✆ | - roadside assistance | 🚴 | Cycle trail | ⊕ | Boat hire | ⊗ | World Heritage site/area |
| ✆ | - emergency | 🚵 | Mountain bike trail | 🦆 | Nature reserve | | |

1 Kilometre = 0.6214 mile
1 metre = 3.2808 feet

## Scale 1:25 000

1 mile = 1.6093 kilometres
100 feet = 30.48 metres

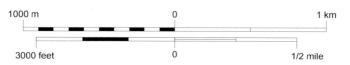

1000 m    0    1 km

3000 feet    0    1/2 mile

**KEY TO MAP PAGES**

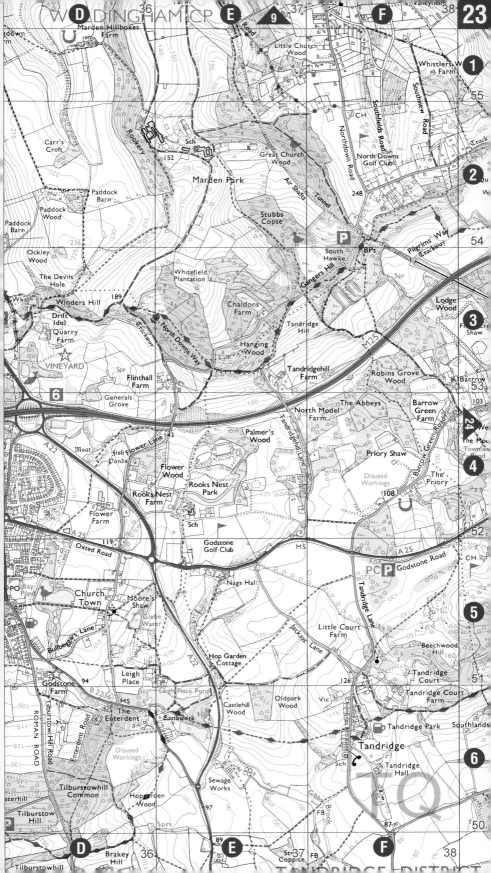

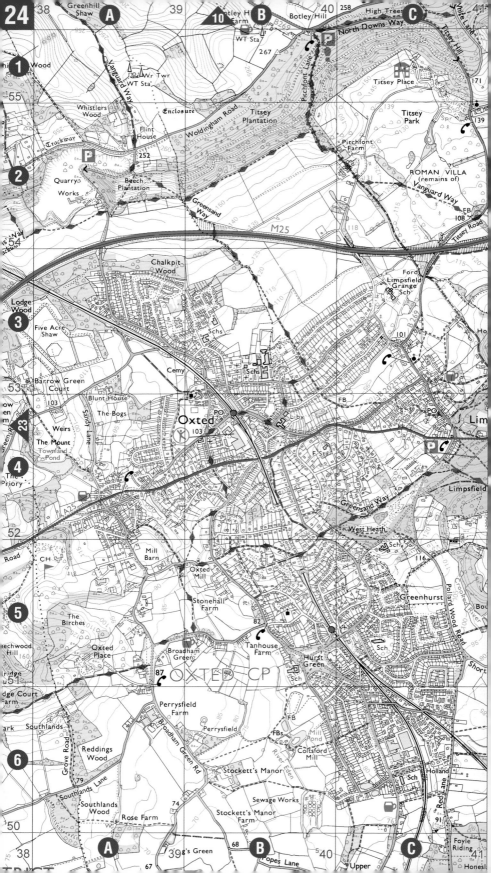

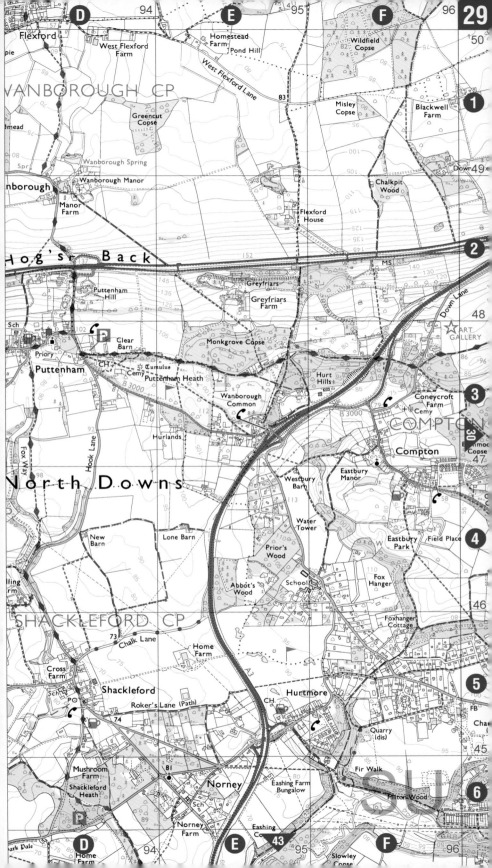

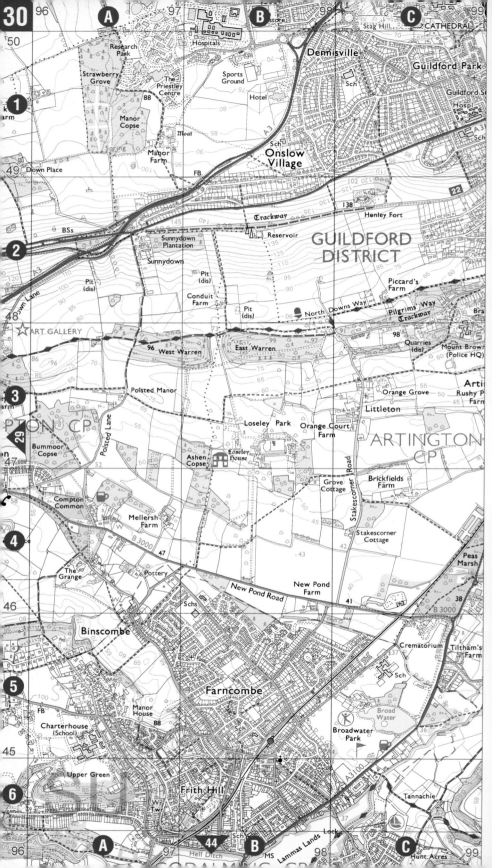

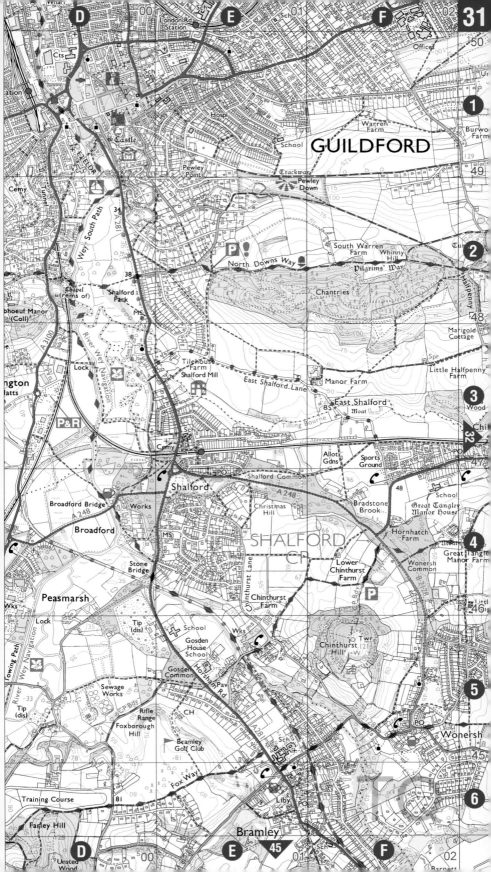

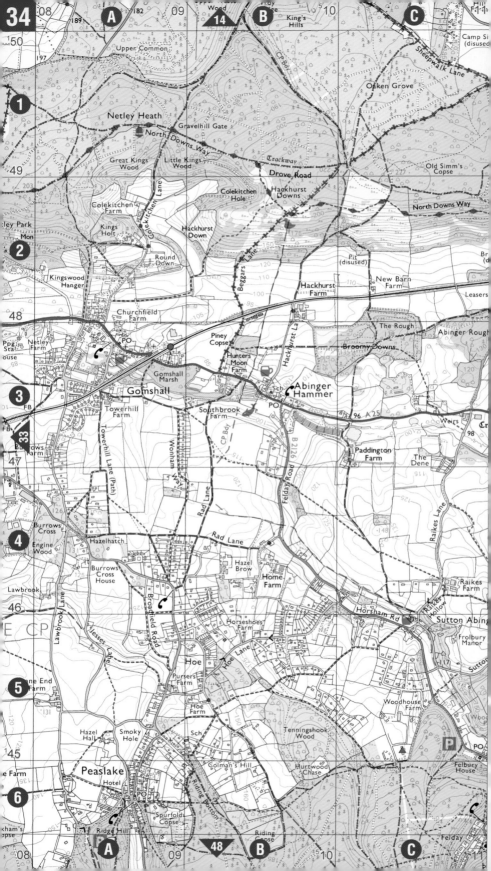

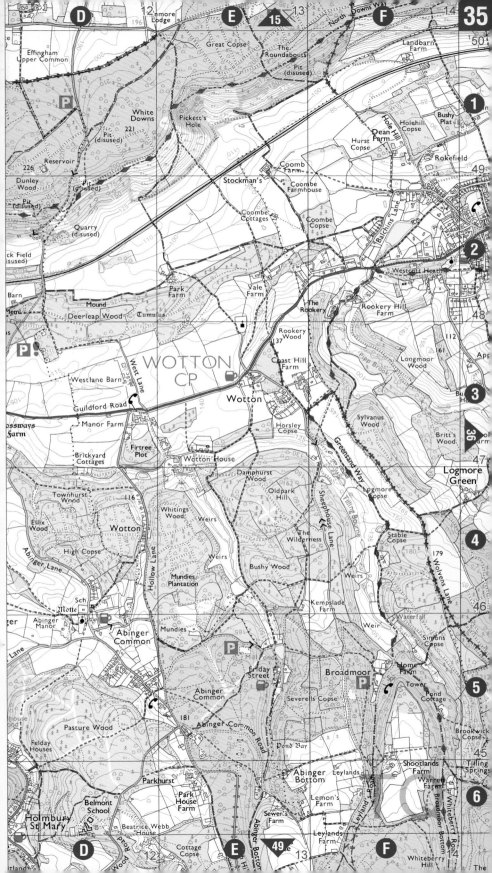

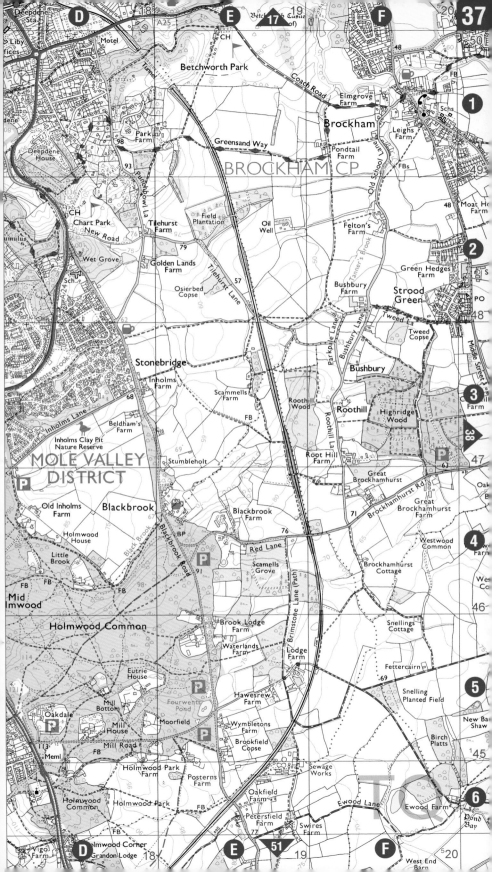

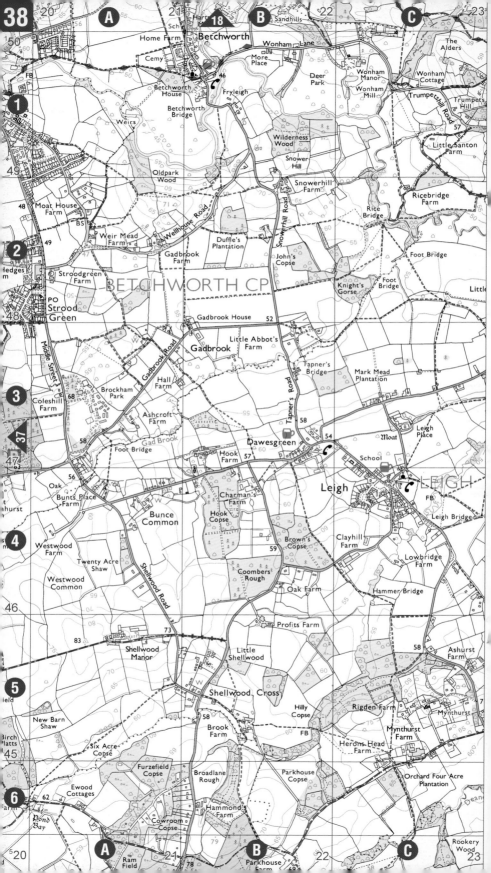

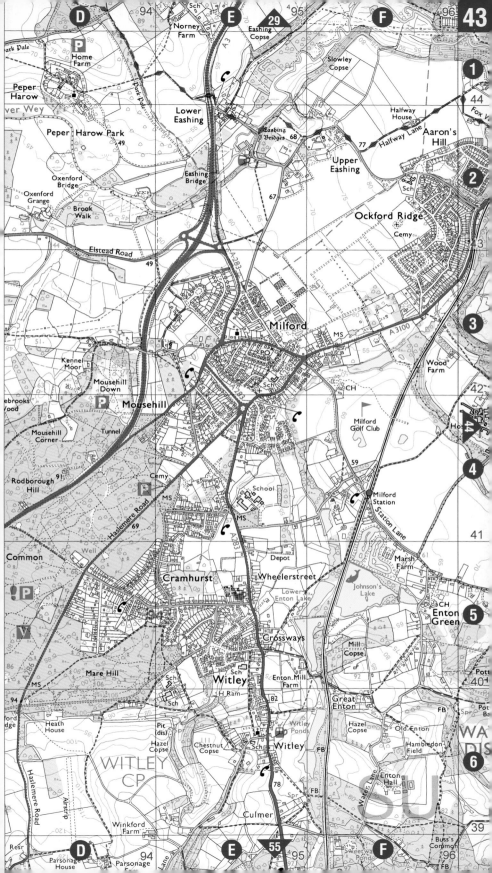

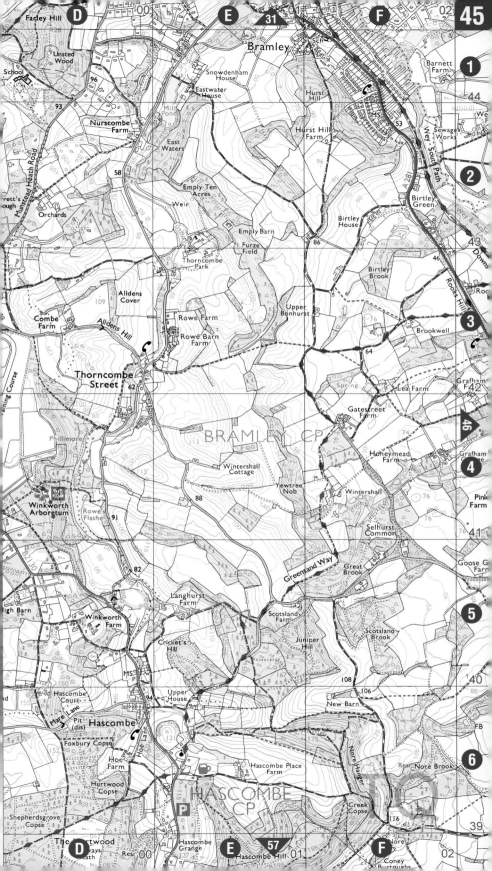

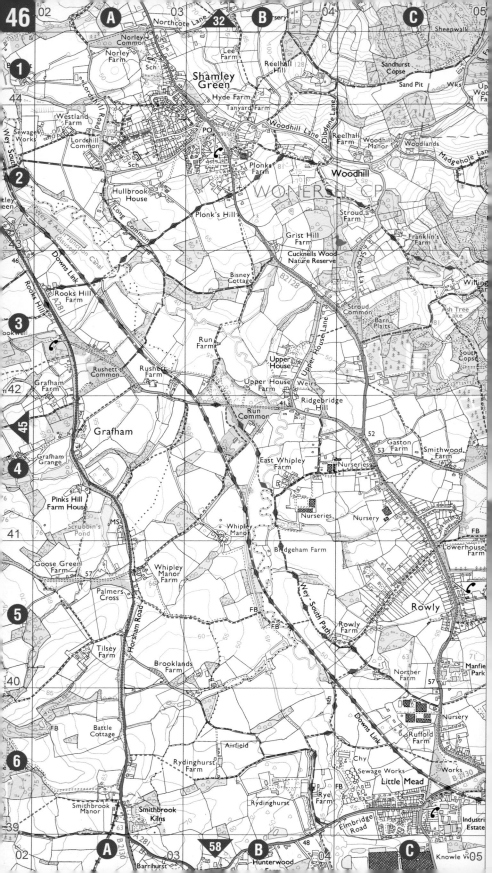

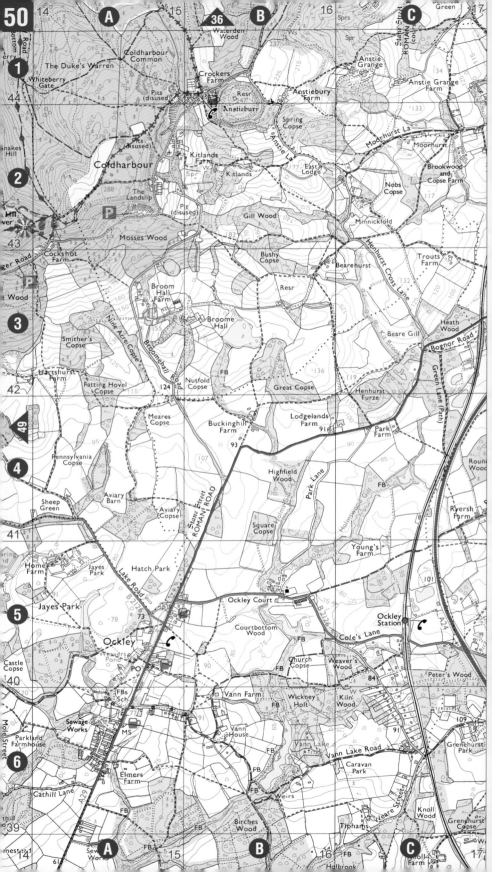

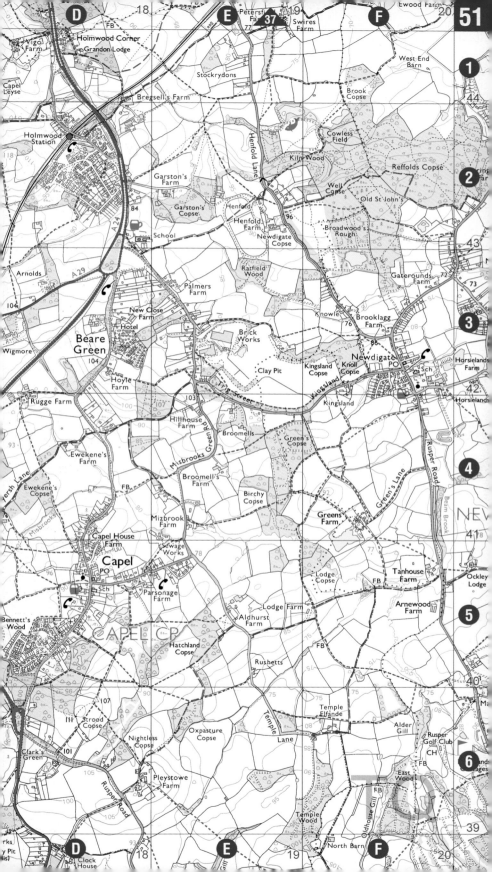

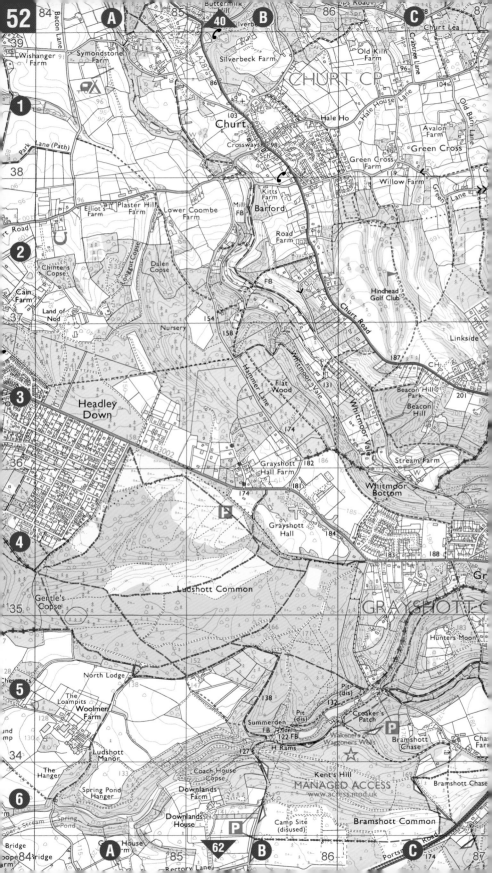

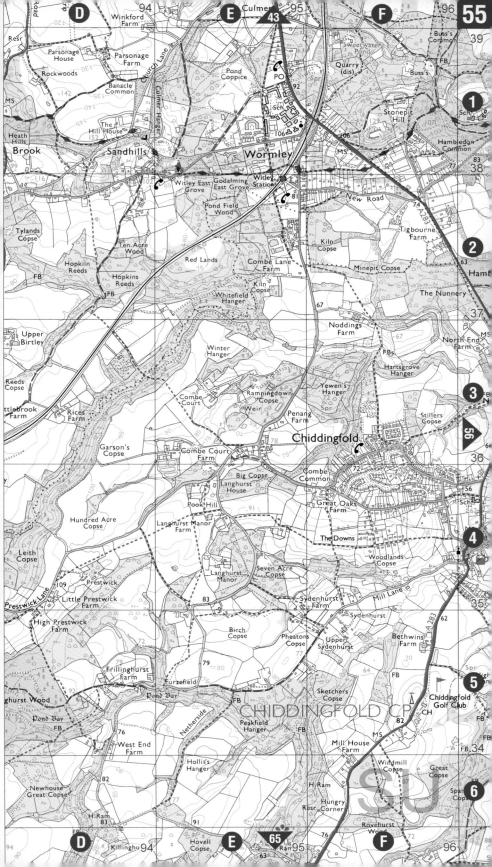

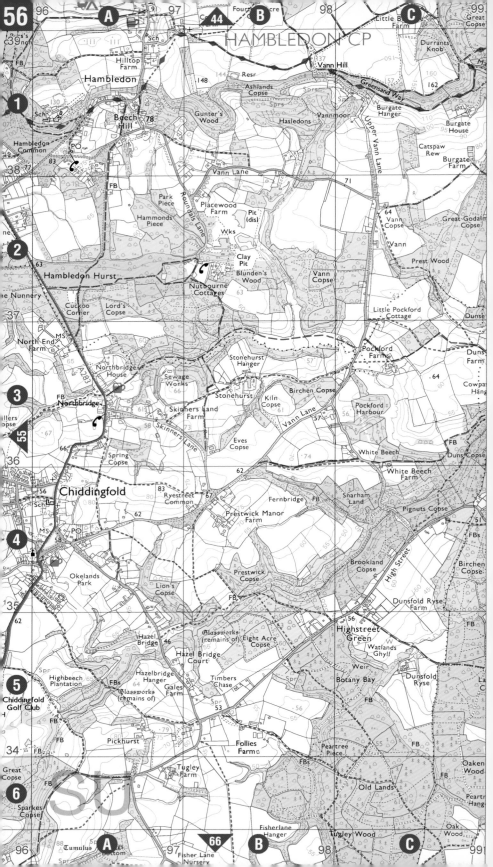

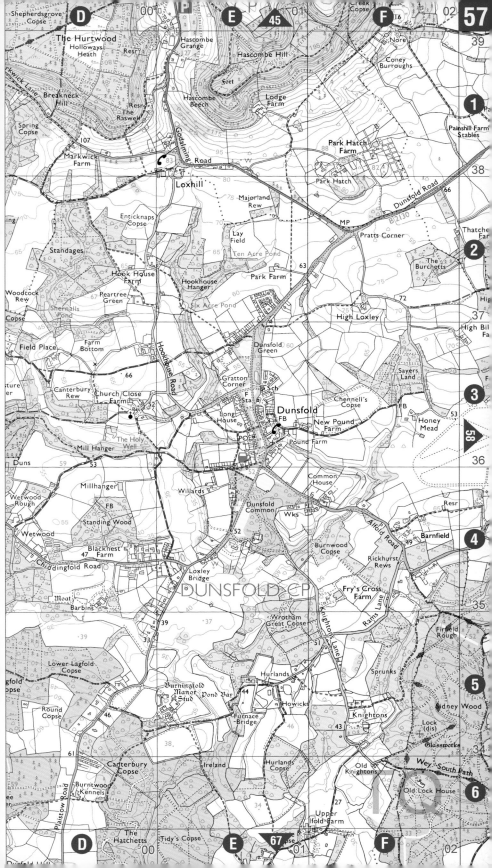

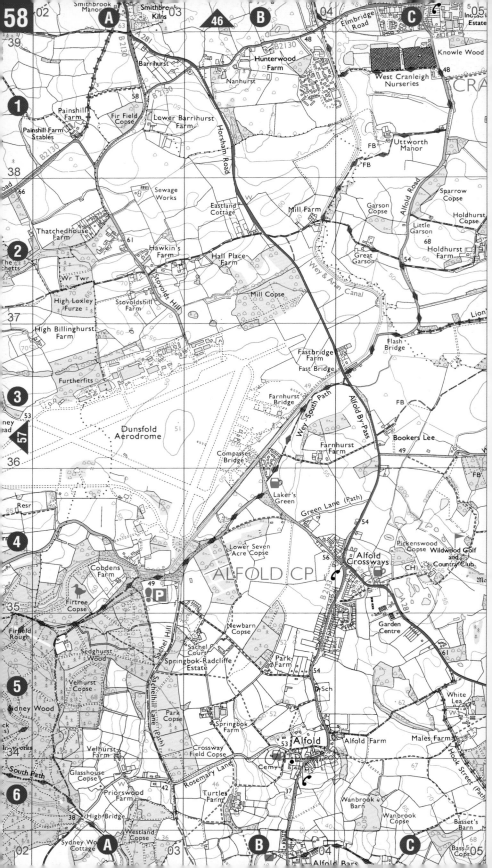

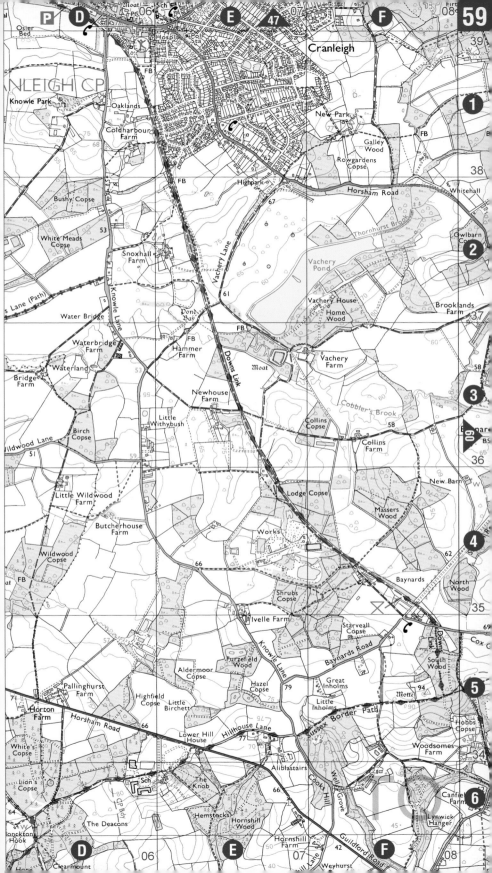

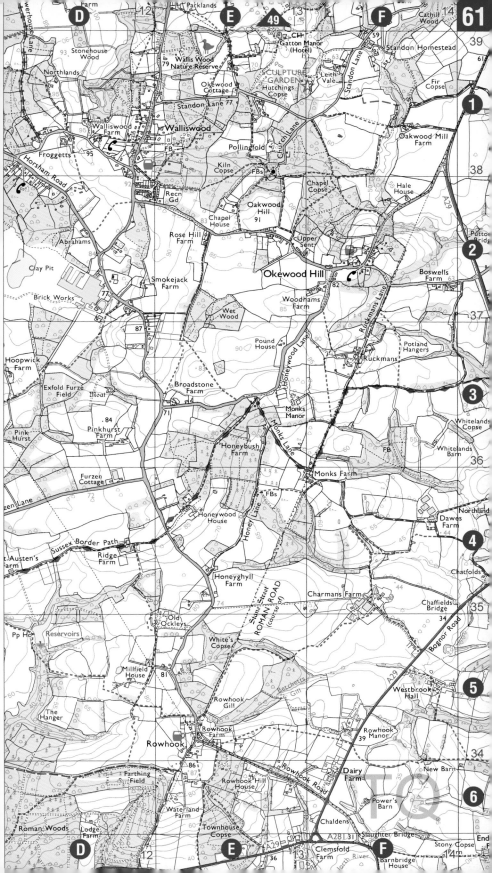

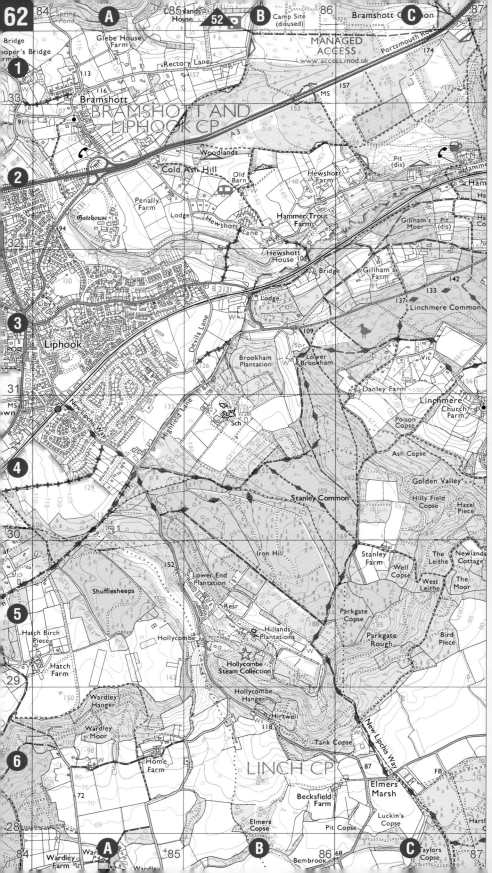

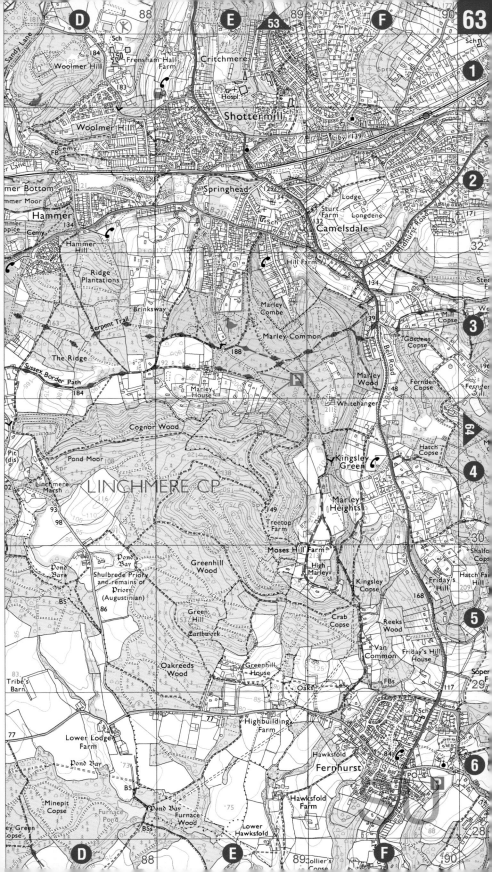

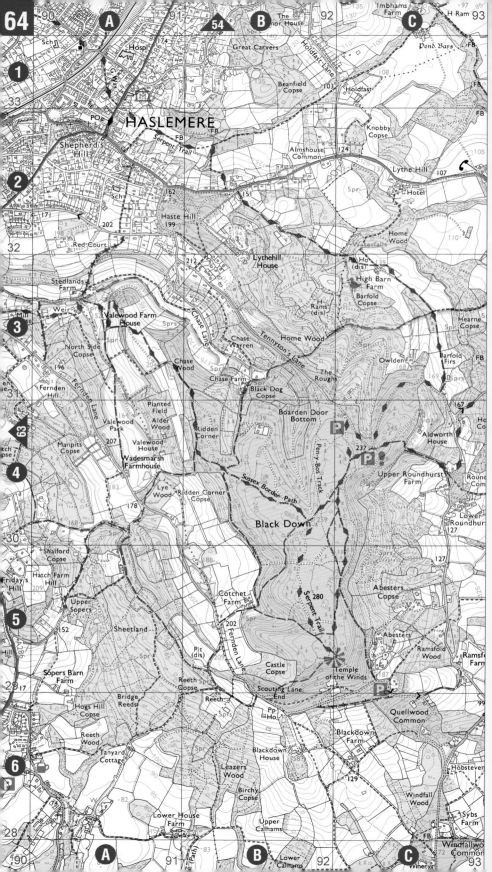

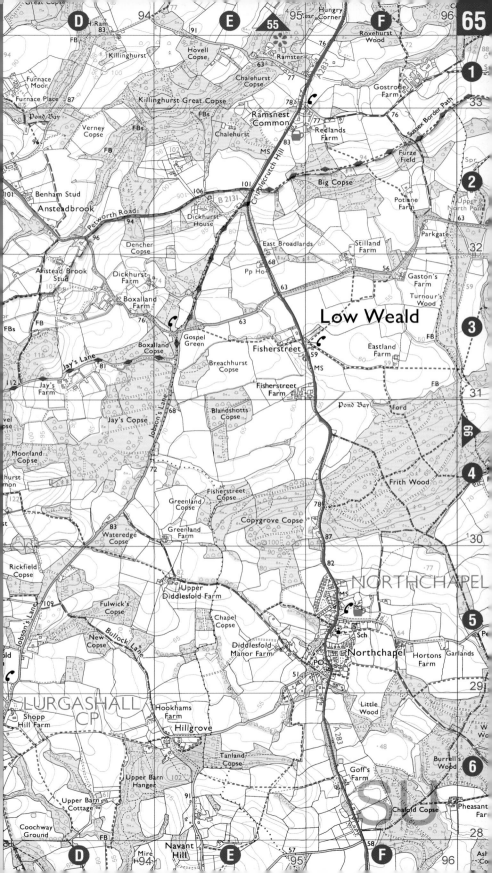

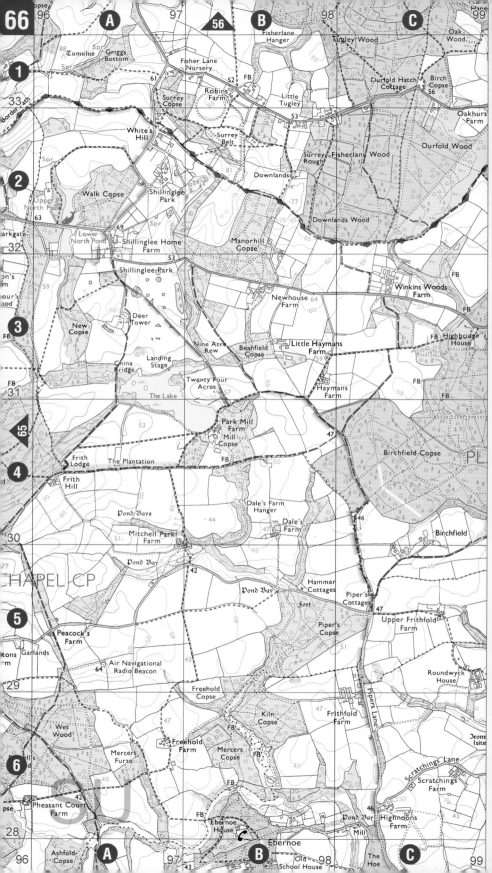

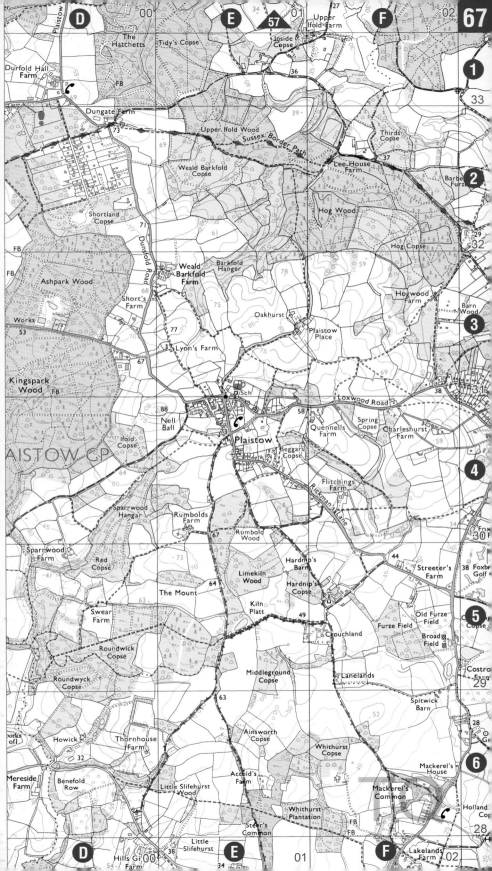

1. The map reference given refers to the actual square in which the feature is located and not the name.

2. A strict alphabetical order is used e.g. Black Lake follows Blackheath Common but precedes Blackshaw Bush

3. Names prefixed with 'The' are indexed under the main name, for example 'The Bourne' appears in the B section.

## THE NATIONAL GRID REFERENCING SYSTEM

The grid lines form part of the National Grid and are at 1 km intervals.

To give a unique reference position of a point to within 100 metres proceed as follows:

Sample point: **Aaron's Hill**

1. Read letters identifying 100,000 metre square in which the point lies (**SU**)

2. FIRST QUOTE EASTINGS - locate the first VERTICAL grid line to LEFT of the point and read the BLUE figures labelling the line in the top or bottom margin of the page (**96**). Estimate tenths from the grid line to the point (**0**). This gives a figure of **960**

3. THEN QUOTE NORTHINGS - locate the first HORIZONTAL grid line BELOW the point and read the BLUE figures labelling the line in the left or right margin of the page (**43**). Estimate tenths from the grid line to the point (**7**). This gives a figure of **437**

Sample Reference: **Aaron's Hill SU 960 437**

A22 Lay-by (S of Caterham)
............3C **22** TQ 349 534
A25 Lay-by (Moorhouse)
............3E **25** TQ 426 533
A25 Lay-by (Tandridge)
............5F **23** TQ 375 518
Aaron's Hill .........2A **44** SU 960 437
Abbot's Wood .......4E **29** SU 944 462
Abesters Copse ......5C **64** SU 923 296
Abinger Bottom .....6E **35** TQ 126 448
Abinger Common ....5D **35** TQ 115 459
............5E **35** TQ 123 454
Abinger Forest .....5B **36** TQ 153 454
Abinger Hammer ....3B **34** TQ 095 474
Abinger Roughs .....3C **34** TQ 108 479
Abinger Roughs Car Park
............3D **35** TQ 110 479
Albury ............3C **32** TQ 049 478
Albury Downs ......1C **32** TQ 043 490
Albury Heath .......4E **33** TQ 061 467
Albury Heath Car Park
............4E **33** TQ 061 466
Albury Park ........3E **33** TQ 063 475
Alderbrook Park .....4D **47** TQ 059 418
Alderstead Heath ....1D **21** TQ 298 552
Alfold ............6B **58** TQ 038 339
Alfold Bars .........6B **58** TQ 036 333
Alfold Crossways ....4C **58** TQ 040 353
Ansteadbrook ......2D **65** SU 930 324
Anstiebury ........2B **50** TQ 153 439
Aperfield .........3E **11** TQ 424 585
Artington .........3D **31** SU 992 476
Artington Park & Ride, Guildford
............3D **31** SU 993 475
Ashcombe Wood ....5B **16** TQ 157 514
Ash Green ........1A **28** SU 902 496
Ashpark Wood .....3D **67** SU 993 317
Ashurst Rough ......4E **17** TQ 186 521

Badshot Lea .......2C **26** SU 864 486
Bagmoor Common ...3C **42** SU 926 422
Bagmoor Common Nature Reserve
............3C **42** SU 926 423
Banstead ..........2A **6** TQ 258 599
Banstead Heath .....1D **19** TQ 233 554
Banstead Wood .....4A **6** TQ 265 578
Banstead Woods Car Park
............3B **6** TQ 273 583
Barfold Copse ......3C **64** SU 921 316
Barfold Copse Nature Reserve
............3C **64** SU 921 317
Barford ...........2B **52** SU 853 377
Barkfold Hanger .....3E **67** TQ 004 319
Barnett Hill ........5A **32** TQ 025 455
Baynard's Park .....3A **60** TQ 081 362
Bay Pond Nature Reserve
............5D **23** TQ 352 516
Beacon Hill ........3C **52** SU 866 364
............3D **53** SU 874 367
Beare Green .......3D **51** TQ 177 423
Beaver Water World ..5C **10** TQ 407 563

Beech Plantation ....2A **24** TQ 386 544
Berry's Green .......2F **11** TQ 438 592
Betchworth ........1B **38** TQ 210 498
Betchworth Bridge ..1B **38** TQ 211 494
Betchworth Park .....1E **37** TQ 183 497
Betchworth Station ..5B **18** TQ 210 513
Big Copse .........2F **65** SU 952 324
Biggin Hill ........2D **11** TQ 418 590
Binscombe ........5A **30** SU 965 452
Birch Copse .......1C **66** SU 986 331
Birchen Copse ......4C **56** SU 988 353
Birches Wood ......6B **50** TQ 154 388
Birchfield Copse .....4C **66** SU 984 306
Birch Wood ........5D **9** TQ 352 565
Birtley Green .......2F **45** TQ 016 433
Black Down ........4B **64** SU 916 301
Black Down, Tennyson's Lane
  Car Park .........4C **64** SU 920 308
Black Down, Tennyson's Lane
  (Lower) Car Park ..4C **64** SU 922 306
Black Hanger .......2A **54** SU 901 377
Blackheath ........4B **32** TQ 031 462
............4B **32** TQ 037 460
Blackheath Common,
  Blackheath Lane Car Park
............4B **32** TQ 036 462
  Littleford Lane Car Park
............5B **32** TQ 034 456
Black Lake .........6C **26** SU 862 445
Blackshaw Bush ....2F **11** TQ 440 592
Bletchingley .......6A **22** TQ 327 507
Bocketts Farm Park ..2B **16** TQ 156 549
Bookham Station ....1E **15** TQ 127 556
Bookham Wood .....3A **16** TQ 146 535
Book Hurst ........6F **47** TQ 075 392
Botany Bay ........5C **56** SU 980 345
Botley Hill .........6B **10** TQ 394 557
Botley Hill Car Park ..1B **24** TQ 398 554
Boundless Copse ....3A **54** SU 901 366
The Bourne ........6A **26** SU 846 448
Bourne Wood ......1B **40** SU 856 443
Bourne Wood Car Park
............6B **26** SU 859 446
Bowles Rough ......1A **60** TQ 083 382
Bowlhead Green ....1B **54** SU 916 382
Boxalland Copse ....3D **65** SU 939 313
Box Hill ...........5D **17** TQ 176 513
............5A **18** TQ 200 517
Boxhill & Westhumble Station
............5C **16** TQ 167 518
Boxhill Bridge .......6E **17** TQ 183 502
Box Hill Country Park
............5E **17** TQ 181 519
Box Hill East Car Park
............5E **17** TQ 181 512
Box Hill Visitor Centre
............5D **17** TQ 178 513
Box Hill Visitor Centre Car Park
............5D **17** TQ 178 513
Bramley ..........6E **31** TQ 008 448
Bramshott .........2A **62** SU 843 328
Bramshott Chase ....6C **52** SU 867 338

Bramshott Common ..6C **52** SU 863 335
Bramshott Common Car Park
............6B **52** SU 855 337
Brewer Street .......5A **22** TQ 323 517
Brickfields Country Park
............1C **26** SU 866 495
Brimmer Car Park (Headley Heath)
............3A **18** TQ 206 532
Britty Wood ........5A **28** SU 903 453
Britty Wood Car Park
............5A **28** SU 904 456
Broadford .........4D **31** SU 997 466
Broadford Bridge ...4D **31** SU 997 467
Broadham Green ....5A **24** TQ 388 512
Broadmoor ........5F **35** TQ 134 455
Broadwater Park ....5C **30** SU 981 451
Broadwood's Rough ..2F **51** TQ 192 430
Brockham ..........1F **37** TQ 197 494
Brook .............4E **33** TQ 060 463
............1D **55** SU 930 380
Brookland Copse ....4C **56** SU 981 353
Broome Park .......6B **18** TQ 215 507
Broomy Downs .....3C **34** TQ 101 478
Buckland ..........6C **18** TQ 221 508
Buckland Hills ......4C **18** TQ 229 525
Buildings Wood .....1C **60** TQ 108 385
Bunce Common .....4A **38** TQ 206 467
Burford Bridge ......5D **17** TQ 171 518
Burntcommon ......2C **12** TQ 040 549
Burnwood Copse ....4F **57** TQ 011 354
Burrell's Wood ......6F **65** SU 959 285
Burrows Cross ......4A **34** TQ 082 465
Bury Hill ..........2B **36** TQ 156 483
Busbridge .........3B **44** SU 979 429
Busbridge Lakes ....3B **44** SU 972 420
Busbridge Woods ...5C **44** SU 980 405
Bushy Hill .........6A **12** TQ 021 509
Bushy Wood ........4E **35** TQ 127 463
Buss's Common .....1F **55** SU 958 389

Camelsdale ........2E **63** SU 889 320
Canterbury Copse ...6D **57** SU 998 339
Capel .............5D **51** TQ 175 406
Castle Hill .........6A **22** TQ 321 507
Caterham ..........1C **22** TQ 342 553
Caterham Station ...1C **22** TQ 341 554
Catteshall .........1C **44** SU 982 442
Chafold Copse ......6F **65** SU 956 281
Chaldon ...........1F **21** TQ 313 550
Chantries .........2F **31** TQ 011 482
Chantries Car Park ..2E **31** TQ 003 483
Chantry Wood ......1E **33** TQ 063 494
Chapel Bank Nature Reserve
............1A **10** TQ 385 607
Chapelhill Wood .....4A **16** TQ 146 522
Charleshill ........1F **41** SU 892 443
Chart Park ........2D **37** TQ 175 486
Chase Wood .......3A **64** SU 909 312
Chelsham .........3F **9** TQ 371 588
Chiddingfold ......4A **56** SU 960 354
Chilworth ........3A **32** TQ 022 470

Chilworth Station . . . . .3B **32**  TQ 031 472
Chinthurst Hill . . . . . . .5F **31**  TQ 012 458
Chinthurst Hill Car Park
. . . . . . . . . . . . . . . . .4F **31**  TQ 013 462
Chinthurst Hill Tower
. . . . . . . . . . . . . . . . .5F **31**  TQ 013 458
Chipstead . . . . . . . . . .3B **6**  TQ 274 583
Chipstead Bottom . . . . .4A **6**  TQ 268 570
Chipstead Station . . . . .3B **6**  TQ 276 582
Church Croft . . . . . . . .4C **28**  SU 921 465
Church Town . . . . . . . .5D **23**  TQ 356 515
Church Wood . . . . . . . .4F **49**  TQ 137 418
Churt . . . . . . . . . . . . .1B **52**  SU 855 381
Churt Common . . . . . . .6B **40**  SU 857 394
Churt Place . . . . . . . . .6D **41**  SU 875 395
Clammer Hill . . . . . . . .5C **54**  SU 921 340
Clandon Downs . . . . . .1D **33**  TQ 053 497
Clandon Park . . . . . . . .5C **12**  TQ 042 512
Clandon Station . . . . . .4C **12**  TQ 045 527
Clark's Green . . . . . . . .6D **51**  TQ 172 396
Cockshot Car Park . . . . .3E **17**  TQ 188 535
Cognor Wood . . . . . . . .4D **63**  SU 879 307
Cold Ash Hill . . . . . . . .2A **62**  SU 848 325
Coldharbour . . . . . . . . .2A **50**  TQ 149 436
Coldharbour Common
. . . . . . . . . . . . . . . . .1A **50**  TQ 147 443
. . . . . . . . . . . . . . . . .2A **50**  TQ 145 435
Colekitchen Hole . . . . .2B **34**  TQ 093 489
Coles Meads . . . . . . . .5B **20**  TQ 276 515
Colley Hill . . . . . . . . . .4E **19**  TQ 244 523
Colyers Hanger . . . . . .2B **32**  TQ 037 481
Combe Bottom . . . . . . .1E **33**  TQ 068 490
Combe Common . . . . . .4F **55**  SU 950 359
Compasses Bridge . . . .3B **58**  TQ 034 360
Compton . . . . . . . . . . .4B **26**  SU 853 465
. . . . . . . . . . . . . . . . .3F **29**  SU 955 470
Compton Common . . . . .4A **30**  SU 962 467
Conyburu Hill . . . . . . . .4D **19**  TQ 234 523
Copygrove Copse . . . . .4E **65**  SU 947 301
Cotts Wood . . . . . . . . .4B **12**  TQ 032 525
Coulsdon . . . . . . . . . . .2D **7**  TQ 297 593
Coulsdon Common
. . . . . . . . . . . . . . . . .5A **8**  TQ 321 569
Coulsdon Common Car Park
. . . . . . . . . . . . . . . . .5F **7**  TQ 316 568
Coulsdon South Station
. . . . . . . . . . . . . . . . .2D **7**  TQ 298 590
Coulsdon Town Station
. . . . . . . . . . . . . . . . .2E **7**  TQ 301 597
Cox Green . . . . . . . . . .5B **60**  TQ 093 347
Craig's Wood . . . . . . . .5E **53**  SU 885 344
Cramhurst . . . . . . . . . .5E **43**  SU 940 408
Cranleigh . . . . . . . . . . .6D **47**  TQ 058 390
Cranleigh, Stockland Square Car Park
. . . . . . . . . . . . . . . . .6D **47**  TQ 054 391
Crockham Hill . . . . . . . .6F **25**  TQ 442 506
Crooksbury Common
. . . . . . . . . . . . . . . . .5E **27**  SU 888 452
Crooksbury Hill . . . . . . .5D **27**  SU 878 459
Crooksbury Hill Car Park
. . . . . . . . . . . . . . . . .5D **27**  SU 878 457
Cucknell's Wood Nature Reserve
. . . . . . . . . . . . . . . . .2C **46**  TQ 040 430
Culmer . . . . . . . . . . . . .6E **43**  SU 948 390
Culverswell Hill . . . . . . .5F **27**  SU 892 459
Cutmill Pond . . . . . . . .5B **28**  SU 912 455

Dabdon Bridge . . . . . . .4E **39**  TQ 247 464
Dawcombe Wood . . . . .4B **18**  TQ 215 524
Dawesgreen . . . . . . . . .3B **38**  TQ 218 471
Dean Hill . . . . . . . . . . .5F **7**  TQ 319 562
Deanoak Bridge . . . . . .3E **39**  TQ 241 457
Deepdene Bridge . . . . .6E **17**  TQ 186 503
Deerleap Wood . . . . . .2D **35**  TQ 115 480
Denbies Hillside Car Park
. . . . . . . . . . . . . . . . .6A **16**  TQ 141 503
Denbies Wine Estate
. . . . . . . . . . . . . . . . .5C **16**  TQ 165 511
Denshire Wood . . . . . .3A **16**  TQ 148 539
Derry's Hill . . . . . . . . . .5B **32**  TQ 032 458
Derry's Wood . . . . . . . .5B **32**  TQ 032 455
The Devil's Jumps . . . . .6C **40**  SU 864 394
Devil's Punch Bowl . . . . .3F **53**  SU 894 360
Devil's Punch Bowl Car Park
. . . . . . . . . . . . . . . . .4F **53**  SU 890 357
Dogkennel Green . . . . .6D **15**  TQ 119 504

Dollyper's Hill Nature Reserve
. . . . . . . . . . . . . . . . .3F **7**  TQ 317 583
Dorking . . . . . . . . . . . .1C **36**  TQ 168 496
Dorking (Deepdene) Station
. . . . . . . . . . . . . . . . .6D **17**  TQ 170 501
Dorking Museum & Heritage Centre
. . . . . . . . . . . . . . . . .1C **36**  TQ 164 494
Dorking Station . . . . . .6D **17**  TQ 171 504
Dorking West Station
. . . . . . . . . . . . . . . . .1B **36**  TQ 159 498
Doversgreen . . . . . . . . .2F **39**  TQ 257 482
Downe Bank Nature Reserve
. . . . . . . . . . . . . . . . .1F **11**  TQ 438 609
Down House . . . . . . . . .1F **11**  TQ 431 611
Downlands Wood . . . . .2C **66**  SU 980 322
Downs Link . . . . . . . . . .4A **32**  TQ 023 464
. . . . . . . . . . . . . . . . .3A **46**  TQ 023 428
. . . . . . . . . . . . . . . . .6C **46**  TQ 042 397
. . . . . . . . . . . . . . . . .3E **59**  TQ 064 366
. . . . . . . . . . . . . . . . .5F **59**  TQ 078 348
Druids Grove . . . . . . . .3B **16**  TQ 157 532
Dunley Wood . . . . . . . .2D **35**  TQ 111 489
Duns Copse . . . . . . . . .3C **56**  SU 988 360
Dunsfold . . . . . . . . . . .3E **57**  TQ 006 362
Dunsfold Aerodrome
. . . . . . . . . . . . . . . . .3A **58**  TQ 026 362
Dunsfold Common . . . . .4E **57**  TQ 006 357
Dunsfold Green . . . . . . .3E **57**  TQ 006 368
Durfold Wood . . . . . . . .2C **66**  SU 986 327

Eashing . . . . . . . . . . . .2E **43**  SU 944 439
Eashing Bridge . . . . . . .2E **43**  SU 943 434
Eashing Bridges . . . . . .2E **43**  SU 946 438
East Clandon . . . . . . . .5E **13**  TQ 060 517
East Horsley . . . . . . . . .2B **14**  TQ 092 542
East Surrey Museum
. . . . . . . . . . . . . . . . .1C **22**  TQ 340 554
Ebernoe . . . . . . . . . . . .6B **66**  SU 973 279
Effingham . . . . . . . . . . .3D **15**  TQ 117 536
Effingham Common . . . .1C **14**  TQ 103 553
Effingham Forest . . . . . .6B **14**  TQ 096 504
Eight Acre Copse . . . . .5B **56**  SU 974 348
Ellen's Green . . . . . . . .4C **60**  TQ 100 354
Elmers Copse . . . . . . . .6B **62**  SU 854 280
Elmers Marsh . . . . . . . .6C **62**  SU 862 283
Elstead . . . . . . . . . . . . .2A **42**  SU 909 436
Elstead Bridge . . . . . . .2A **42**  SU 905 438
Elstead Common . . . . .3A **42**  SU 904 420
Elstead Moat Car Park
. . . . . . . . . . . . . . . . .4F **41**  SU 899 416
Elstead Road, Seale Car Park
. . . . . . . . . . . . . . . . .4F **27**  SU 894 464
Enton Green . . . . . . . . .5F **43**  SU 957 406
Etherley Copse . . . . . . .4E **49**  TQ 127 417
Ewhurst . . . . . . . . . . . .5B **48**  TQ 090 405
Ewhurst Green . . . . . . .6B **48**  TQ 094 395

Fairdean Downs . . . . . .3D **7**  TQ 298 580
Farleigh . . . . . . . . . . . .1E **9**  TQ 368 602
Farley Common . . . . . . .3F **25**  TQ 436 539
Farley Green . . . . . . . . .5D **33**  TQ 059 453
Farley Heath . . . . . . . . .6D **33**  TQ 053 449
Farley Heath
   (Hurtwood 8) Car Park
. . . . . . . . . . . . . . . . .6D **33**  TQ 050 448
Farley Hill . . . . . . . . . . .1D **45**  SU 993 444
Farm Park . . . . . . . . . .5B **58**  TQ 037 342
Farncombe . . . . . . . . . .5B **30**  SU 974 450
Farncombe Station . . . . .5B **30**  SU 976 451
Farnham . . . . . . . . . . . .4A **26**  SU 840 465
Farnham Heath Nature Reserve
. . . . . . . . . . . . . . . . .2C **40**  SU 861 438
Farnham Maltings . . . . .4A **26**  SU 840 465
Farnham Park . . . . . . . .2A **26**  SU 840 480
Farnham Park Car Park
. . . . . . . . . . . . . . . . .3A **26**  SU 838 475
Farnham Station . . . . . .4A **26**  SU 844 465
Farnhurst Bridge . . . . . .3B **58**  TQ 037 364
Farthing Downs . . . . . . .3D **7**  TQ 299 580
Farthing Downs Car Park
. . . . . . . . . . . . . . . . .4E **7**  TQ 301 571
Fast Bridge . . . . . . . . . .3C **58**  TQ 040 366
Felbury House
   (Hurtwood 9) Car Park
. . . . . . . . . . . . . . . . .5C **34**  TQ 108 450

Fernden Lane Car Park
. . . . . . . . . . . . . . . . .5C **64**  SU 923 290
Fernhurst . . . . . . . . . . .6F **63**  SU 896 284
Fernhurst Centre Car Park
. . . . . . . . . . . . . . . . .6F **63**  SU 895 284
Fetcham . . . . . . . . . . . .1A **16**  TQ 147 556
Fetcham Downs . . . . . .2B **16**  TQ 153 542
Fickleshole . . . . . . . . . .1A **10**  TQ 389 603
Fir Tree Copse Nature Reserve
. . . . . . . . . . . . . . . . .4A **58**  TQ 022 351
Fisherlane Wood . . . . . .2C **66**  SU 980 326
Fisherstreet . . . . . . . . . .3F **65**  SU 950 313
Flanchford Bridge . . . . .3D **39**  TQ 234 479
Flash Bridge . . . . . . . . .3C **58**  TQ 043 369
The Flashes Nature Reserve
. . . . . . . . . . . . . . . . .6C **40**  SU 865 398
Flat Wood . . . . . . . . . . .3B **52**  SU 856 365
Flexford . . . . . . . . . . . .1C **28**  SU 928 498
The Forest (Effingham) Nature Reserve
. . . . . . . . . . . . . . . . .1B **14**  TQ 095 551
Forest Green . . . . . . . . .4E **49**  TQ 123 413
Forked Pond . . . . . . . . .4B **42**  SU 918 411
Foxley Wood Nature Reserve
. . . . . . . . . . . . . . . . .1F **7**  TQ 314 607
Freehold Wood . . . . . . .4A **16**  TQ 144 520
Frensham . . . . . . . . . . .4A **40**  SU 846 415
Frensham Common . . . . .5B **40**  SU 852 408
Frensham Common,
   Great Pond Car Park
. . . . . . . . . . . . . . . . .5A **40**  SU 843 405
Frensham Common,
   Little Pond Car Park
. . . . . . . . . . . . . . . . .4B **40**  SU 857 418
Frensham Common,
   Priory Lane Car Park
. . . . . . . . . . . . . . . . .4B **40**  SU 853 416
Frensham Great Pond
. . . . . . . . . . . . . . . . .5A **40**  SU 845 401
Frensham Little Pond
. . . . . . . . . . . . . . . . .4B **40**  SU 858 414
Friday Street . . . . . . . . .5E **35**  TQ 127 456
Friday Street Car Park
. . . . . . . . . . . . . . . . .5E **35**  TQ 125 457
Frillinghurst Wood . . . . .5D **55**  SU 930 343
Frith Hill . . . . . . . . . . . .6B **30**  SU 970 446
Frith Wood . . . . . . . . . .4F **65**  SU 956 304
Frithys Wood . . . . . . . .3B **12**  TQ 033 530
Furnace Pond . . . . . . . .6D **63**  SU 878 281
Furnace Wood . . . . . . . .6E **63**  SU 882 281
Furzefield Wood . . . . . .1C **54**  SU 924 383

Gadbrook . . . . . . . . . . .3B **38**  TQ 210 478
Garson's Copse . . . . . . .3D **55**  SU 935 361
Gason Wood . . . . . . . . .4E **13**  TQ 065 529
Gatton . . . . . . . . . . . . .3B **20**  TQ 276 532
Gatwick . . . . . . . . . . . .6B **28**  SU 915 448
General's Pond . . . . . . .4B **28**  SU 910 462
Gentle's Copse . . . . . . .4A **52**  SU 839 351
Gibbet Hill . . . . . . . . . .4F **53**  SU 899 359
Gillham's Moor . . . . . . .2C **62**  SU 864 321
Givons Grove . . . . . . . .2D **17**  TQ 172 545
Godalming . . . . . . . . . .2B **44**  SU 970 438
Godalming Museum
. . . . . . . . . . . . . . . . .2A **44**  SU 968 437
Godalming Station . . . . .2A **44**  SU 966 439
Godstone . . . . . . . . . . .5C **22**  TQ 349 517
Godstone Farm & Playbarn
. . . . . . . . . . . . . . . . .5D **23**  TQ 352 510
Golden Valley . . . . . . . .3D **53**  SU 877 361
Gomshall . . . . . . . . . . .3A **34**  TQ 085 478
Gomshall Station . . . . . .3A **34**  TQ 089 478
Goodley Stock . . . . . . .4F **25**  TQ 439 521
Gosden Common . . . . . .5E **31**  TQ 001 456
Gospel Green . . . . . . . .3E **65**  SU 941 314
Graeme Hendry Wood Nature Reserve
. . . . . . . . . . . . . . . . .6C **22**  TQ 347 505
Grafham . . . . . . . . . . . .4A **46**  TQ 022 417
Gravelly Hill . . . . . . . . .3B **22**  TQ 337 532
Grayshott . . . . . . . . . . .4D **53**  SU 873 353
Grayshott Pottery . . . . .4D **53**  SU 870 355
Grayswood . . . . . . . . . .5B **54**  SU 917 346
Grayswood Common
. . . . . . . . . . . . . . . . .5B **54**  SU 915 340
Great Bookham . . . . . . .2F **15**  TQ 135 544
Great Bookham Common,
   Tunnel Car Park . . . . .1F **15**  TQ 130 557

| | | |
|---|---|---|
| Great Church Wood . . . .2E **23** | TQ 368 546 | |
| Great Copse . . . . . . . . .1E **35** | TQ 124 499 | |
| Great Godalming Copse | | |
| . . . . . . . . . . . . . . . .2C **56** | SU 988 376 | |
| Great Hurst Wood . . . .1B **18** | TQ 211 554 | |
| Greatlee Wood . . . . . . .2C **14** | TQ 105 545 | |
| Great Ridings Plantation | | |
| . . . . . . . . . . . . . . . .2C **14** | TQ 105 540 | |
| Green Cross . . . . . . . . .1C **52** | SU 864 380 | |
| Greencut Copse . . . . . .1D **29** | SU 939 493 | |
| Greenhill Wood . . . . . .5E **63** | SU 883 298 | |
| Greensand Way . . . . . .6C **22** | TQ 345 499 | |
| . . . . . . . . . . . . . . . .4C **24** | TQ 402 521 | |
| . . . . . . . . . . . . . . . .4F **25** | TQ 432 520 | |
| . . . . . . . . . . . . . . . .3F **35** | TQ 132 470 | |
| . . . . . . . . . . . . . . . .1E **37** | TQ 185 491 | |
| . . . . . . . . . . . . . . . .1D **39** | TQ 238 495 | |
| . . . . . . . . . . . . . . . .6A **42** | SU 904 392 | |
| . . . . . . . . . . . . . . . .5E **45** | SU 009 407 | |
| . . . . . . . . . . . . . . . .3E **47** | TQ 065 425 | |
| . . . . . . . . . . . . . . . .2C **48** | TQ 107 437 | |
| . . . . . . . . . . . . . . . .2F **49** | TQ 132 431 | |
| . . . . . . . . . . . . . . . .4F **53** | SU 892 355 | |
| . . . . . . . . . . . . . . . .1C **56** | SU 982 385 | |
| Guildford . . . . . . . . . . .1D **31** | TQ 998 495 | |
| Guildford, Artington Park & Ride | | |
| . . . . . . . . . . . . . . . .3D **31** | SU 993 474 | |
| Guildford Castle . . . . . .1D **31** | TQ 997 492 | |
| Guildford Cathedral . . .1C **30** | SU 985 500 | |
| Guildford, Merrow Park & Ride | | |
| . . . . . . . . . . . . . . . .6B **12** | TQ 033 507 | |
| Guildford Museum . . . . .1D **31** | SU 996 492 | |
| Guildford Park . . . . . . .1C **30** | SU 988 496 | |
| Guildford Station . . . . .1D **31** | SU 991 495 | |
| Guildford Tourist Information Centre | | |
| . . . . . . . . . . . . . . . .1D **31** | SU 998 494 | |
| The Gullet . . . . . . . . . .5E **7** | TQ 302 563 | |
| Hackhurst Downs . . . . .2B **34** | TQ 096 488 | |
| Hackhurst Downs Nature Reserve | | |
| . . . . . . . . . . . . . . . .2B **34** | TQ 096 486 | |
| Hale . . . . . . . . . . . . . .2A **26** | SU 848 484 | |
| Halnacker Copse . . . . .2B **54** | SU 913 375 | |
| Hambledon . . . . . . . . . .1A **56** | SU 965 385 | |
| Hambledon Common | | |
| . . . . . . . . . . . . . . . .1F **55** | SU 959 382 | |
| Hambledon Hurst . . . . .2A **56** | SU 962 373 | |
| Hammer . . . . . . . . . . .2D **63** | SU 875 321 | |
| Hammer Bottom . . . . . .2D **63** | SU 870 324 | |
| Hammer Bridge . . . . . .4C **38** | TQ 222 461 | |
| Hammer Pond . . . . . . .5B **42** | SU 915 402 | |
| Hampton Park . . . . . . .4A **28** | SU 905 464 | |
| Hamsey Green . . . . . . .2C **8** | TQ 349 595 | |
| Hangers Wood . . . . . . .5C **14** | TQ 101 513 | |
| Hankley Common . . . . .4E **41** | SU 880 415 | |
| Hankley Common Car Park | | |
| . . . . . . . . . . . . . . . .5F **41** | SU 892 406 | |
| Hannah Peschar Sculpture Garden | | |
| . . . . . . . . . . . . . . . .1F **61** | TQ 130 386 | |
| Happy Valley . . . . . . . .5E **7** | TQ 308 568 | |
| Hascombe . . . . . . . . . .6D **45** | SU 999 398 | |
| Hascombe Hill . . . . . . .1E **57** | TQ 007 387 | |
| Hascombe Hill Car Park | | |
| . . . . . . . . . . . . . . . .6E **45** | TQ 001 391 | |
| Hascombe Hill (Fort) | | |
| . . . . . . . . . . . . . . . .1E **57** | TQ 004 386 | |
| Haslemere . . . . . . . . . .2A **64** | SU 904 328 | |
| Haslemere Educational Museum | | |
| . . . . . . . . . . . . . . . .1A **64** | SU 906 330 | |
| Haslemere Station . . . . .2F **63** | SU 897 329 | |
| Haste Hill . . . . . . . . . . .2A **64** | SU 909 322 | |
| Hatch Farm Hill . . . . . .5A **64** | SU 900 296 | |
| Hatchlands Park . . . . . .4E **13** | TQ 067 520 | |
| Hawley's Corner . . . . . .5F **11** | TQ 434 568 | |
| Hazel Bridge . . . . . . . .5A **56** | SU 968 348 | |
| Hazelbridge Hanger . . .5A **56** | SU 966 346 | |
| Headley . . . . . . . . . . . .2A **18** | TQ 206 544 | |
| Headley Down . . . . . . .3A **52** | SU 838 365 | |
| Headley Heath . . . . . . .3A **18** | TQ 202 535 | |
| Headley Heath (Brimmer) Car Park | | |
| . . . . . . . . . . . . . . . .3A **18** | TQ 205 532 | |
| Headley Heath Main Car Park | | |
| . . . . . . . . . . . . . . . .3A **18** | TQ 205 538 | |
| Hearne Copse . . . . . . .3C **64** | SU 928 315 | |
| Heath End . . . . . . . . . .1A **26** | SU 847 493 | |
| Heath Hills . . . . . . . . . .1D **55** | SU 931 382 | |

| | | |
|---|---|---|
| Heronswood Mere . . . .3D **21** | TQ 299 535 | |
| High Button . . . . . . . . .3A **54** | SU 907 361 | |
| The High Chart . . . . . . .4F **25** | TQ 432 523 | |
| Highcomb Bottom . . . . .2F **53** | SU 895 375 | |
| Highcomb Copse . . . . . .2E **53** | SU 888 372 | |
| Highridge Wood . . . . . .3F **37** | TQ 196 473 | |
| Highridge Wood Car Park | | |
| . . . . . . . . . . . . . . . .4F **37** | TQ 199 469 | |
| Highstreet Green . . . . .5C **56** | SU 980 349 | |
| High Wethersell Wood | | |
| . . . . . . . . . . . . . . . .4F **47** | TQ 071 417 | |
| Hillgrove . . . . . . . . . . .6E **65** | SU 941 287 | |
| Hindhead . . . . . . . . . . .4E **53** | SU 888 357 | |
| Hindhead Common . . . .3F **53** | SU 893 361 | |
| Hindhead Youth Hostel | | |
| . . . . . . . . . . . . . . . .3F **53** | SU 892 368 | |
| Hoe . . . . . . . . . . . . . . .5B **34** | SU 091 456 | |
| The Hoe . . . . . . . . . . . .6C **66** | SU 982 278 | |
| Hog Copse . . . . . . . . . .2F **67** | TQ 018 320 | |
| Hog's Back . . . . . . . . . .2D **29** | SU 933 483 | |
| Hog's Back Car Park | | |
| . . . . . . . . . . . . . . . .2C **28** | TQ 927 482 | |
| Hog Wood . . . . . . . . . .2F **67** | TQ 011 322 | |
| Holland . . . . . . . . . . . .6C **24** | TQ 403 505 | |
| Holloway Hill . . . . . . . .3A **44** | SU 969 429 | |
| Hollycombe . . . . . . . . .5B **62** | SU 854 292 | |
| Holly Lane Car Park . . . .3B **6** | TQ 272 583 | |
| Holmbury Hill . . . . . . . .2C **48** | TQ 104 432 | |
| Holmbury Hill (Fort) | | |
| . . . . . . . . . . . . . . . .2C **48** | TQ 104 430 | |
| Holmbury Hill | | |
| (Hurtwood 1) Car Park | | |
| . . . . . . . . . . . . . . . .2B **48** | TQ 098 431 | |
| Holmbury St Mary . . . .6D **35** | TQ 110 446 | |
| Holmbury Youth Hostel | | |
| . . . . . . . . . . . . . . . .5C **34** | TQ 104 450 | |
| Holmen's Grove . . . . . .3C **54** | SU 922 361 | |
| Holmethorpe . . . . . . . .5C **20** | TQ 286 517 | |
| Holmwood Common | | |
| . . . . . . . . . . . . . . . .5D **37** | TQ 175 459 | |
| Holmwood Common, Fourwents Pond | | |
| (Blackbrook Road) Car Park | | |
| . . . . . . . . . . . . . . . .5E **37** | TQ 183 454 | |
| Holmwood Common, Fourwents Pond | | |
| (Mill Road) Car Park | | |
| . . . . . . . . . . . . . . . .5E **37** | TQ 182 452 | |
| Holmwood Common, | | |
| Inholms Lane Car Park | | |
| . . . . . . . . . . . . . . . .4D **37** | TQ 170 469 | |
| Holmwood Common, | | |
| Mill Road Car Park | | |
| . . . . . . . . . . . . . . . .5D **37** | TQ 173 451 | |
| Holmwood Common, | | |
| Scamells Car Park . . . .4E **37** | TQ 182 462 | |
| Holmwood Corner . . . .1D **51** | TQ 173 444 | |
| Holmwood Station . . . .2D **51** | TQ 174 437 | |
| Holt Wood . . . . . . . . . .2F **9** | TQ 377 593 | |
| Home Pond . . . . . . . . .5B **42** | SU 919 408 | |
| Home Wood . . . . . . . . .3B **64** | SU 916 313 | |
| Hook Wood . . . . . . . . .6F **13** | TQ 078 507 | |
| Hooley . . . . . . . . . . . . .5C **6** | TQ 287 565 | |
| Horsley Station . . . . . . .2B **14** | TQ 092 545 | |
| Houndown . . . . . . . . . .5F **41** | SU 894 404 | |
| Hovel Copse . . . . . . . . .4C **64** | SU 929 308 | |
| Hoyle . . . . . . . . . . . . . .3D **51** | TQ 175 424 | |
| Hungry Hill . . . . . . . . . .1A **26** | SU 844 497 | |
| Hurlands . . . . . . . . . . .5E **57** | TQ 005 348 | |
| Hurlands Copse . . . . . .6E **57** | TQ 008 339 | |
| Hurst Green . . . . . . . . .5B **24** | TQ 398 512 | |
| Hurst Green Station . . .5B **24** | TQ 399 513 | |
| Hurst Hill . . . . . . . . . . .1F **45** | TQ 010 440 | |
| Hurthill Copse . . . . . . .4A **54** | SU 909 358 | |
| Hurtmore . . . . . . . . . . .5F **29** | SU 950 453 | |
| Hurt Wood . . . . . . . . . .2A **48** | TQ 084 438 | |
| The Hurtwood . . . . . . .1D **57** | SU 995 389 | |
| Hyde Hill . . . . . . . . . . .2E **53** | SU 883 377 | |
| Hydestile . . . . . . . . . . .5A **44** | SU 968 406 | |
| Hydon Heath . . . . . . . .6B **44** | SU 977 398 | |
| Hydon Heath Car Park | | |
| . . . . . . . . . . . . . . . .5B **44** | SU 978 402 | |
| Hydon's Ball . . . . . . . . .6B **44** | SU 977 395 | |
| Inholms Clay Pit Nature Resverve | | |
| . . . . . . . . . . . . . . . .3D **37** | TQ 175 472 | |
| Invall . . . . . . . . . . . . . .4A **54** | SU 904 352 | |
| Iron Hill . . . . . . . . . . . .5B **62** | SU 855 299 | |

| | | |
|---|---|---|
| Irons Bottom . . . . . . . .4F **39** | TQ 250 463 | |
| Itchingwood Common | | |
| . . . . . . . . . . . . . . . .6D **25** | TQ 415 507 | |
| Jayes Park . . . . . . . . . .5A **50** | TQ 141 405 | |
| Jay's Copse . . . . . . . . .4D **65** | SU 937 308 | |
| Johnson's Lake . . . . . . .5F **43** | SU 953 406 | |
| Juniper Hill . . . . . . . . . .4D **19** | TQ 237 521 | |
| Juniperhill Wood . . . . . .4D **17** | TQ 173 529 | |
| Juniper Top . . . . . . . . . .4E **17** | TQ 183 524 | |
| Juniper Valley . . . . . . . .5C **44** | SU 982 406 | |
| Kenley . . . . . . . . . . . . .1A **8** | TQ 325 600 | |
| Kenley Aerodrome . . . .4A **8** | TQ 327 579 | |
| Kenley Common . . . . . .3B **8** | TQ 331 586 | |
| Kenley Station . . . . . . .1A **8** | TQ 324 601 | |
| Kent Hatch . . . . . . . . . .5F **25** | TQ 438 517 | |
| Kent's Hill . . . . . . . . . . .6C **52** | SU 860 338 | |
| Kettlebury Hill . . . . . . .5D **41** | SU 879 404 | |
| Killinghurst Great Copse | | |
| . . . . . . . . . . . . . . . .1E **65** | SU 941 330 | |
| Kiln Copse . . . . . . . . . .6B **66** | SU 975 288 | |
| King's Hills . . . . . . . . . .6B **14** | TQ 097 500 | |
| Kingsley Green . . . . . . .4F **63** | SU 895 305 | |
| Kingspark Wood . . . . . .3D **67** | SU 991 311 | |
| Kings Wood . . . . . . . . .1D **9** | TQ 352 604 | |
| Kitchen Copse . . . . . . .4A **22** | TQ 328 524 | |
| Lagfold Copse . . . . . . .5D **57** | SU 990 345 | |
| The Lake . . . . . . . . . . .3A **66** | SU 968 310 | |
| Laker's Green . . . . . . . .4B **58** | TQ 035 358 | |
| Lammas Lands . . . . . . .1B **44** | SU 977 443 | |
| Lawbrook Lane, Peaslake | | |
| (Hurtwood 10) Car Park | | |
| . . . . . . . . . . . . . . . .2A **48** | TQ 081 438 | |
| Leazers Wood . . . . . . .6B **64** | SU 913 284 | |
| Leigh . . . . . . . . . . . . . .4C **38** | TQ 223 469 | |
| Leigh Bridge . . . . . . . . .4C **38** | TQ 226 466 | |
| Leith Copse . . . . . . . . .4D **55** | SU 931 353 | |
| Leith Hill . . . . . . . . . . .2F **49** | TQ 136 432 | |
| Leith Hill, Broadmoor Car Park | | |
| . . . . . . . . . . . . . . . .5F **35** | TQ 132 454 | |
| Leith Hill, Etherley Copse Car Park | | |
| . . . . . . . . . . . . . . . .4E **49** | TQ 125 416 | |
| Leith Hill, Landslip Car Park | | |
| . . . . . . . . . . . . . . . .2A **50** | TQ 146 432 | |
| Leith Hill Place . . . . . . .3F **49** | TQ 134 428 | |
| Leith Hill Place Wood | | |
| . . . . . . . . . . . . . . . .3F **49** | TQ 136 426 | |
| Leith Hill, Rhododendron Wood Car Park | | |
| . . . . . . . . . . . . . . . .3F **49** | TQ 131 427 | |
| Leith Hill, Starveall Corner Car Park | | |
| . . . . . . . . . . . . . . . .2F **49** | TQ 130 432 | |
| Leith Hill Tower . . . . . .2F **49** | TQ 139 431 | |
| Leith Hill, Windy Gap Car Park | | |
| . . . . . . . . . . . . . . . .3F **49** | TQ 138 428 | |
| Leith Hill Wood . . . . . . .3E **49** | TQ 129 424 | |
| Limekiln Wood . . . . . . .5E **67** | TQ 006 297 | |
| Limpsfield . . . . . . . . . .4C **24** | TQ 406 529 | |
| Limpsfield Chart . . . . . .5E **25** | TQ 426 518 | |
| Limpsfield Chart Golf Club | | |
| . . . . . . . . . . . . . . . .4D **25** | TQ 412 526 | |
| Limpsfield Chart, High Chart Car Park | | |
| . . . . . . . . . . . . . . . .4E **25** | TQ 426 520 | |
| Limpsfield Chart, Moorhouse Car Park | | |
| . . . . . . . . . . . . . . . .4F **25** | TQ 430 529 | |
| Limpsfield Chart, New Road Car Park | | |
| . . . . . . . . . . . . . . . .4C **24** | TQ 409 525 | |
| Limpsfield Chart, Pine Wood Car Park | | |
| . . . . . . . . . . . . . . . .4E **25** | TQ 426 521 | |
| Limpsfield Chart, Ridlands Grove Car Park | | |
| . . . . . . . . . . . . . . . .4D **25** | TQ 418 521 | |
| Limpsfield Chart, | | |
| Scearn Bank (East) Car Park | | |
| . . . . . . . . . . . . . . . .5F **25** | TQ 431 516 | |
| Limpsfield Chart, | | |
| Scearn Bank (West) Car Park | | |
| . . . . . . . . . . . . . . . .5E **25** | TQ 428 517 | |
| Limpsfield Common . . .4C **24** | TQ 409 523 | |
| Linchmere . . . . . . . . . .4C **62** | SU 869 309 | |
| Linchmere Common . . .3C **62** | SU 866 315 | |
| Linchmere Common Nature Reserve | | |
| . . . . . . . . . . . . . . . .3C **62** | SU 861 314 | |
| Lion's Copse . . . . . . . . .4A **56** | SU 968 351 | |

Liphook . . . . . . . . . . .3A **62** SU 839 315
Liphook Station . . . . .4A **62** SU 841 309
Little Bookham . . . . . .1E **15** TQ 126 550
Little Common . . . . . .3B **28** SU 919 475
Little London . . . . . . .4E **33** TQ 065 467
Littleton . . . . . . . . . .3C **30** SU 981 474
Lockner Bridge . . . . . .3B **32** TQ 036 473
Logmore Green . . . . . .4A **36** TQ 141 468
London Biggin Hill Airport
. . . . . . . . . . . . . . . .1D **11** TQ 415 609
London Loop . . . . . . . .1C **6** TQ 284 606
. . . . . . . . . . . . . . . .3D **7** TQ 299 585
. . . . . . . . . . . . . . . .5F **7** TQ 314 567
. . . . . . . . . . . . . . . .2B **8** TQ 336 598
. . . . . . . . . . . . . . . .3B **8** TQ 331 588
. . . . . . . . . . . . . . . .1D **9** TQ 358 602
London Road (Guildford) Station
. . . . . . . . . . . . . . . .1E **31** TQ 002 500
Lordshill Common . . .2A **46** TQ 024 437
Loseley House . . . . . . .3B **30** SU 974 470
Loseley Park . . . . . . . .3B **30** SU 975 473
Lower Bourne . . . . . . .6B **26** SU 850 447
Lower Canfold Wood
. . . . . . . . . . . . . . . .6A **48** TQ 082 393
Lower Enton Lake . . . .5F **43** SU 950 405
Lower Kingswood . . .3E **19** TQ 248 538
Lower Lagfold Copse
. . . . . . . . . . . . . . . .5D **57** SU 994 346
Lower Puttenham Common
. . . . . . . . . . . . . . . .5A **28** SU 908 454
Loxhill . . . . . . . . . . . .1E **57** TQ 001 380
Loxley Bridge . . . . . . .4E **57** TQ 002 353
Ludshott Common . . .4B **52** SU 850 351
Ludshott Common Car Park
. . . . . . . . . . . . . . . .4B **52** SU 852 357
Lumberdine Wood . . .4B **10** TQ 393 575
Luxted . . . . . . . . . . . .1F **11** TQ 433 602
Lythe Hill . . . . . . . . . .2C **64** SU 923 325

Mackerel's Common . .6F **67** TQ 017 282
Manorhill Copse . . . . .2B **66** SU 974 320
Manpits Copse . . . . . .4A **64** SU 901 306
Marchant's Hill . . . . .2D **53** SU 878 372
Marden Park Car Park
. . . . . . . . . . . . . . . .2F **23** TQ 373 541
Marden Park Nature Reserve
. . . . . . . . . . . . . . . .2E **23** TQ 369 540
Mare Hill . . . . . . . . . .5D **43** SU 935 400
Margery . . . . . . . . . . .4F **19** TQ 253 528
Margery Wood . . . . . .4E **19** TQ 245 525
Margery Wood Car Park
. . . . . . . . . . . . . . . .4E **19** TQ 245 527
Marley Common . . . . .3E **63** SU 888 314
Marley Common Car Park
. . . . . . . . . . . . . . . .3E **63** SU 886 311
Marley Heights . . . . . .4F **63** SU 891 302
Marley Wood . . . . . . .3F **63** SU 893 311
Massers Wood . . . . . .4F **59** TQ 075 356
Mayes Green . . . . . . . .6E **49** TQ 121 393
Mercers Copse . . . . . .6B **66** SU 972 285
Mercers Park Country Park
. . . . . . . . . . . . . . . .4E **21** TQ 300 520
Mercers Park Country Park Car Park
. . . . . . . . . . . . . . . .5E **21** TQ 300 517
Merrow . . . . . . . . . . .6A **12** TQ 027 506
Merrow Common . . . . .5A **12** TQ 027 516
Merrow Downs . . . . . .1B **32** TQ 033 498
Merrow Park & Ride, Guildford
. . . . . . . . . . . . . . . .6B **12** TQ 033 507
Merstham . . . . . . . . . .3D **21** TQ 290 532
Merstham Station . . .3D **21** TQ 291 532
Mickleham . . . . . . . . .3D **17** TQ 170 533
Mickleham Downs . . .3D **17** TQ 177 535
Middle Bourne . . . . . .5A **26** SU 841 450
Mid Holmwood . . . . .4C **36** SU 168 461
Milford . . . . . . . . . . . .3E **43** SU 946 423
Milford Common Car Park
. . . . . . . . . . . . . . . .4E **43** SU 940 413
Milford Station . . . . . .4F **43** SU 954 413
Millbridge . . . . . . . . . .3A **40** SU 848 423
Mill Copse . . . . . . . . .2B **58** TQ 035 371
Mill Plain,
  Pitch Hill (Hurtwood 3) Car Park
. . . . . . . . . . . . . . . .3F **47** TQ 079 426
Milton Bridge . . . . . . .2B **36** TQ 151 487
Milton Heath . . . . . . . .2B **36** TQ 154 488

Milton Heath Car Park
. . . . . . . . . . . . . . . .2B **36** TQ 154 488
Milton Wood . . . . . . . .6F **29** SU 956 447
Minepit Copse . . . . . . .2F **55** SU 954 373
. . . . . . . . . . . . . . . .6D **63** SU 873 282
Mitchley Wood . . . . . . .1B **8** TQ 335 605
The Moat . . . . . . . . . .4A **42** SU 900 415
The Moat Car Park . . .4F **41** SU 899 416
Mogador . . . . . . . . . .4D **19** TQ 239 529
Mole Gap Trail . . . . . .1C **16** TQ 164 555
. . . . . . . . . . . . . . . .6C **16** TQ 162 506
Mollards Wood . . . . . .3C **10** TQ 402 588
Moorhouse . . . . . . . . .3E **25** TQ 429 533
Moorhouse Bank . . . . .3F **25** TQ 430 532
Moorland Copse . . . . .4D **65** SU 931 306
Moor Park . . . . . . . . . .4C **26** SU 869 464
Moor Park Nature Reserve
. . . . . . . . . . . . . . . .5C **26** SU 868 458
Mosses Wood . . . . . . .2A **50** TQ 146 430
Mountain Wood . . . . . .6B **14** TQ 091 507
Mousehill . . . . . . . . . .4E **43** SU 945 415
Mousehill Down . . . . .3D **43** SU 936 420
Mousehill Down Car Park
. . . . . . . . . . . . . . . .4D **43** SU 937 418
Mugswell . . . . . . . . . .2F **19** TQ 258 546
Mundies Plantation . . .4E **35** TQ 121 462
Munstead Heath . . . . .3C **44** SU 985 425

Nags Wood . . . . . . . . .2C **60** TQ 102 372
Naldersworth . . . . . . . .5D **39** TQ 231 452
Navant Hill . . . . . . . . .6E **65** SU 943 279
Netherlands . . . . . . . . .1D **33** TQ 055 499
Netherne-on-the-Hill . . .5D **7** TQ 295 564
Netley Heath . . . . . . . .1A **34** SU 086 493
Netley Park . . . . . . . . .2F **33** TQ 077 486
Newdigate . . . . . . . . . .3F **51** TQ 196 421
Newlands Corner . . . . .1C **32** TQ 044 491
Newlands Corner,
  Albury Downs Car Park
. . . . . . . . . . . . . . . .1C **32** TQ 042 492
Newlands Corner Visitor Centre
. . . . . . . . . . . . . . . .1C **32** TQ 043 492
Newlands Corner, White Lane Car Park
. . . . . . . . . . . . . . . .1B **32** TQ 032 490
New Pond . . . . . . . . . .5B **42** SU 919 404
Norbury Park . . . . . . . .3B **16** TQ 157 534
Norbury Park, Crabtree Lane Car Park
. . . . . . . . . . . . . . . .4B **16** TQ 158 524
Norbury Park, Fetcham Car Park
. . . . . . . . . . . . . . . .2B **16** TQ 151 548
Norbury Park, Young Street Car Park
. . . . . . . . . . . . . . . .1C **16** TQ 163 551
Norcote Wood . . . . . . .4D **13** TQ 054 525
Nore Hill . . . . . . . . . . .4A **10** TQ 383 573
Norley Common . . . . . .1A **46** TQ 026 444
Norney . . . . . . . . . . . .6E **29** SU 940 447
Northbridge . . . . . . . . .3A **56** SU 964 363
Northchapel . . . . . . . . .5F **65** SU 952 294
North Downs Way . . . .6C **10** TQ 401 555
. . . . . . . . . . . . . . . .6F **11** TQ 432 559
. . . . . . . . . . . . . . . .6F **15** TQ 133 500
. . . . . . . . . . . . . . . .5C **16** TQ 161 514
. . . . . . . . . . . . . . . .4C **18** TQ 227 524
. . . . . . . . . . . . . . . .5F **19** TQ 254 514
. . . . . . . . . . . . . . . .4A **20** TQ 265 525
. . . . . . . . . . . . . . . .2A **22** TQ 323 540
. . . . . . . . . . . . . . . .3E **23** TQ 361 534
. . . . . . . . . . . . . . . .4C **26** SU 865 467
. . . . . . . . . . . . . . . .3B **28** SU 914 473
. . . . . . . . . . . . . . . .2C **30** SU 980 480
. . . . . . . . . . . . . . . .2E **31** TQ 007 483
. . . . . . . . . . . . . . . .2B **32** TQ 033 487
. . . . . . . . . . . . . . . .1E **33** TQ 060 491
. . . . . . . . . . . . . . . .1A **34** TQ 089 492
. . . . . . . . . . . . . . . .2C **34** TQ 106 487
North Holmwood . . . . .3C **36** TQ 168 472
The Nower . . . . . . . . . .2B **36** TQ 157 484
Nower Wood . . . . . . . .2F **17** TQ 194 548
Nower Wood Car Park
. . . . . . . . . . . . . . . .2F **17** TQ 193 546
Nutcombe . . . . . . . . . .5E **53** SU 881 342
Nutcombe Down . . . . .4E **53** SU 885 350
Nutcombe Valley . . . . .5E **53** SU 885 348
Nutfield . . . . . . . . . . . .6E **21** TQ 307 505
Nutfield Marsh . . . . . . .5E **21** TQ 300 516
Nut Wood . . . . . . . . . .4A **20** TQ 266 520

Oaken Grove . . . . . . . .1C **34** TQ 103 496
Oaken Wood . . . . . . . .6C **56** SU 989 339
Oakreeds Wood . . . . . .5E **63** SU 881 291
Ockford Ridge . . . . . . .2F **43** SU 958 431
Ockley . . . . . . . . . . . .5A **50** TQ 147 400
Ockley Common . . . . .4B **42** SU 911 417
Ockley Station . . . . . . .5C **50** TQ 164 404
Okewood Hill . . . . . . . .2F **61** TQ 132 373
Old Coulsdon . . . . . . . .4F **7** TQ 313 574
Old Kiln Museum (Rural Life Centre)
. . . . . . . . . . . . . . . .2B **40** SU 858 433
Old Lands . . . . . . . . . .6C **56** SU 982 337
Oldlands Wood . . . . . .4C **14** TQ 105 520
Old Park Wood . . . . . . .3B **22** TQ 335 536
Onslow Village . . . . . .1B **30** SU 978 492
Oxenford Bridge . . . . .2D **43** SU 935 434
Oxted . . . . . . . . . . . . .4B **24** TQ 392 528
Oxted Station . . . . . . . .4B **24** TQ 393 528
Oyster Hill . . . . . . . . . .2A **18** TQ 201 549

Pains Hill . . . . . . . . . .5D **25** TQ 411 517
Palmers Cross . . . . . . .5A **46** TQ 026 407
Park Copse . . . . . . . . .2C **54** SU 924 375
Park Downs . . . . . . . . .3A **6** TQ 265 584
Parkgate Copse . . . . . .5C **62** SU 861 295
Parkgate Rough . . . . . .5C **62** SU 863 293
Parklands . . . . . . . . . . .6E **49** TQ 124 397
Pasture Wood . . . . . . .5D **35** TQ 114 452
. . . . . . . . . . . . . . . .2D **49** TQ 117 439
Pea Bridge . . . . . . . . . .1C **26** SU 867 490
Peakfield Hanger . . . . .5E **55** SU 946 342
Peaslake . . . . . . . . . . .6A **34** TQ 086 448
Peasmarsh . . . . . . . . . .4C **30** SU 989 462
Peper Harow . . . . . . . .1D **43** SU 932 442
Peper Harow Park . . . .2D **43** SU 935 437
Pewley Down . . . . . . . .2E **31** TQ 009 489
Pickett's Hole . . . . . . . .1E **35** TQ 122 493
Pignuts Copse . . . . . . .4C **56** SU 985 356
Piles Wood . . . . . . . . . .5F **7** TQ 312 560
Pilgrims' Way . . . . . . .6A **16** TQ 149 501
. . . . . . . . . . . . . . . .6E **17** TQ 184 508
. . . . . . . . . . . . . . . .5A **18** TQ 205 513
. . . . . . . . . . . . . . . .5D **19** TQ 235 519
. . . . . . . . . . . . . . . .4B **20** TQ 273 529
. . . . . . . . . . . . . . . .2F **23** TQ 378 540
. . . . . . . . . . . . . . . .1D **25** TQ 418 554
. . . . . . . . . . . . . . . .3F **27** SU 892 478
. . . . . . . . . . . . . . . .2C **30** SU 985 480
. . . . . . . . . . . . . . . .2F **31** TQ 014 484
. . . . . . . . . . . . . . . .2B **32** TQ 039 485
. . . . . . . . . . . . . . . .2F **33** TQ 077 484
Piper's Copse . . . . . . . .5B **66** SU 979 294
Pitchers Wood . . . . . . .5B **10** TQ 397 560
Pitch Hill . . . . . . . . . . .3A **48** TQ 082 423
Pitch Hill (Hurtwood 3) Car Park
. . . . . . . . . . . . . . . .3F **47** TQ 079 426
Pitch Place . . . . . . . . . .6F **41** SU 891 392
Pixham . . . . . . . . . . . .6D **17** TQ 176 502
Plaistow . . . . . . . . . . .4E **67** TQ 004 308
Polecat Valley . . . . . . .5E **53** SU 888 345
Polesden Lacey . . . . . .4F **15** TQ 135 521
Pollard Corner . . . . . . .3D **49** TQ 114 425
Pollingford Bridge . . . .4B **60** TQ 098 359
Pond Copse . . . . . . . . .4C **54** SU 921 356
Pond Hill . . . . . . . . . . .1E **29** SU 945 497
Pot Common . . . . . . . .3A **42** SU 902 428
Potter's Hill . . . . . . . . .5A **44** SU 961 401
Prestwick Copse . . . . .4B **56** SU 974 352
The Pride of the Valley Sculpture Park
. . . . . . . . . . . . . . . .6D **41** SU 871 394
Prior's Wood . . . . . . . .4E **29** SU 947 464
Pudmore Pond . . . . . . .4A **42** SU 906 416
Puttenham . . . . . . . . . .3D **29** SU 932 478
Puttenham Camping Barn
. . . . . . . . . . . . . . . .3D **29** SU 932 479
Puttenham Car Park . . .3D **29** SU 935 477
Puttenham Common
. . . . . . . . . . . . . . . .4B **28** SU 915 466
Puttenham Common Middle Car Park
. . . . . . . . . . . . . . . .5B **28** SU 911 457
Puttenham Common Tarn Car Park
. . . . . . . . . . . . . . . .5B **28** SU 910 455
Puttenham Common Top Car Park
. . . . . . . . . . . . . . . .4C **28** SU 920 461
Puttenham Heath . . . . .3E **29** SU 940 476

Quarry Hangers . . . . . .3A **22**  TQ 320 536
Quarry Hangers Nature Reserve
. . . . . . . . . . . . . . . . . .3F **21**  TQ 318 536
Quarry Hill . . . . . . . . . .4A **20**  TQ 263 521
Quellwood Common . . .6C **64**  SU 924 288

Radnor Road, Peaslake
  (Hurtwood 11) Car Park
. . . . . . . . . . . . . . . . . .2B **48**  TQ 091 439
Ramsnest Common . . .1E **65**  SU 949 330
Ramster . . . . . . . . . . .1E **65**  SU 948 333
Ranmore Common . . . .6F **15**  TQ 137 509
. . . . . . . . . . . . . . . . . .6A **16**  TQ 145 504
Ranmore Common Car Park
. . . . . . . . . . . . . . . . . .6E **15**  TQ 126 501
Redhill . . . . . . . . . . . .6B **20**  TQ 279 506
Redhill Station . . . . . .6C **20**  TQ 281 506
Redlands Wood . . . . . .5C **36**  TQ 163 455
Reedham Station . . . . .1E **7**  TQ 308 607
Reeks Wood . . . . . . . .5F **63**  SU 895 294
Reeth Copse . . . . . . . .5B **64**  SU 910 290
Reffolds Copse . . . . . .2F **51**  TQ 197 435
Reigate . . . . . . . . . . . .6F **19**  TQ 253 502
Reigate Heath  . . . . . .6D **19**  TQ 237 503
Reigate Heath Car Park
. . . . . . . . . . . . . . . . . .6D **19**  TQ 239 502
Reigate Heath Nature Reserve
. . . . . . . . . . . . . . . . . .6D **19**  TQ 236 504
Reigate Hill . . . . . . . . .5F **19**  TQ 256 519
Reigate Park . . . . . . . .1E **39**  TQ 249 495
Reigate Priory Museum
. . . . . . . . . . . . . . . . . .6F **19**  TQ 253 500
Reigate Station . . . . . .6F **19**  TQ 254 507
Reynard's Hill (Hurtwood 12) Car Park
. . . . . . . . . . . . . . . . . .3F **47**  TQ 071 424
Rice Bridge  . . . . . . . .2C **38**  TQ 223 487
Riddlesdown . . . . . . . .1A **8**  TQ 325 603
Riddlesdown Car Park
. . . . . . . . . . . . . . . . . .1A **8**  TQ 325 604
Riddlesdown Station . . .1A **8**  TQ 325 609
The Ridge . . . . . . . . . .3D **63**  SU 875 313
The Ridge (Woldingham) Car Park
. . . . . . . . . . . . . . . . . .2A **24**  TQ 384 546
River Mole . . . . . . . . .4C **16**  TQ 163 524
. . . . . . . . . . . . . . . . . .3D **39**  TQ 237 475
River Wey . . . . . . . . . .2D **43**  SU 931 439
River Wey Navigation
. . . . . . . . . . . . . . . . . .3D **31**  SU 995 477
. . . . . . . . . . . . . . . . . .5D **31**  SU 990 456
River Wey (North Branch)
. . . . . . . . . . . . . . . . . .4C **26**  SU 863 461
River Wey (South Branch)
. . . . . . . . . . . . . . . . . .3B **40**  SU 856 421
Rodborough Common Car Park
. . . . . . . . . . . . . . . . . .4D **43**  SU 937 418
Rodborough Hill . . . . . .4D **43**  SU 931 414
Roman Woods . . . . . . .6D **61**  TQ 112 335
Rose Hill . . . . . . . . . . .2C **36**  TQ 165 489
Roundhurst Common
. . . . . . . . . . . . . . . . . .4C **64**  SU 929 304
Roundwick Copse . . . .5D **67**  SU 997 292
Rowgardens Copse . . .1F **59**  TQ 071 381
Rowhill Nature Reserve
. . . . . . . . . . . . . . . . . .1B **26**  SU 852 497
Rowhill Nature Reserve Car Park
. . . . . . . . . . . . . . . . . .1A **26**  SU 849 499
Rowhook . . . . . . . . . . .5E **61**  TQ 122 341
Rowly . . . . . . . . . . . . .5C **46**  TQ 047 406
Royal Common . . . . . .3C **42**  SU 922 426
Rudgwick . . . . . . . . . .6A **60**  TQ 086 333
Ruffet & Big Wood Nature Reserve
. . . . . . . . . . . . . . . . . .1C **6**  TQ 281 603
Run Common . . . . . . .4B **46**  TQ 034 418
Runfold . . . . . . . . . . . .3D **27**  SU 870 475
Rural Life Centre (Old Kiln Museum)
. . . . . . . . . . . . . . . . . .2B **40**  SU 858 433
Rushett Common . . . . .3A **46**  TQ 024 421
Rushmoor . . . . . . . . . .5D **41**  SU 873 405
Ryka's Café Car Park
. . . . . . . . . . . . . . . . . .4D **17**  TQ 171 520

St Martha's Hill . . . . . .2A **32**  TQ 028 483
St Martha's Hill,
  Guildford Lane Car Park
. . . . . . . . . . . . . . . . . .2B **32**  TQ 035 485

St Martha's Hill,
  Halfpenny Lane Car Park
. . . . . . . . . . . . . . . . . .2A **32**  TQ 021 483
Salomons' Memorial (Mon.)
. . . . . . . . . . . . . . . . . .5D **17**  TQ 179 511
Saltbox Hill Nature Reserve
. . . . . . . . . . . . . . . . . .1C **10**  TQ 408 609
Sanderstead . . . . . . . . .1C **8**  TQ 340 611
Sandhills . . . . . . . . . . .2D **55**  SU 939 379
The Sands  . . . . . . . . .4E **27**  SU 881 465
Sandy Cross . . . . . . . .3E **27**  SU 885 477
Sayers Croft . . . . . . . .5A **48**  TQ 085 402
Sayers Croft Nature Reserve
. . . . . . . . . . . . . . . . . .5A **48**  TQ 084 405
Seale . . . . . . . . . . . . . .3F **27**  SU 896 478
Sedghurst Wood  . . . . .5A **58**  TQ 024 347
Selhurst Common . . . . .4F **45**  TQ 016 410
Send . . . . . . . . . . . . . .1A **12**  TQ 026 555
Serpent Trail . . . . . . . .2A **64**  SU 909 327
. . . . . . . . . . . . . . . . . .5B **64**  SU 918 295
Severalls Copse . . . . . .5E **35**  TQ 129 454
Shackleford  . . . . . . . . .5D **29**  SU 934 454
Shackleford Heath . . . .6D **29**  SU 935 447
Shackleford Heath Car Park
. . . . . . . . . . . . . . . . . .6D **29**  SU 934 445
Shalford . . . . . . . . . . . .4E **31**  TQ 002 469
Shalford Common . . . . .4E **31**  TQ 007 469
Shalford Mill . . . . . . . . .3E **31**  TQ 000 476
Shalford Station . . . . . .3E **31**  TQ 002 471
Shamley Green . . . . . . .2B **46**  TQ 031 438
Sheephatch Copse . . . .6C **26**  SU 869 449
The Sheepleas . . . . . . .5A **14**  TQ 088 515
Sheepleas, Green Dene Car Park
. . . . . . . . . . . . . . . . . .6B **14**  TQ 090 509
Sheepleas, Shere Road Car Park
. . . . . . . . . . . . . . . . . .5A **14**  TQ 084 514
Sheepleas, West Horsley Church Car Park
. . . . . . . . . . . . . . . . . .4A **14**  TQ 088 526
Shellwood Cross  . . . . .5B **38**  TQ 211 454
Sherbourne Farm . . . . .2E **33**  TQ 061 485
Sherbourne Pond Car Park
. . . . . . . . . . . . . . . . . .2D **33**  TQ 059 484
Shere  . . . . . . . . . . . . .3F **33**  TQ 073 478
Shere Heath (Hurtwood 7) Car Park
. . . . . . . . . . . . . . . . . .4F **33**  TQ 071 469
Shere Museum . . . . . . .3F **33**  TQ 072 477
Shillinglee Park . . . . . .3A **66**  SU 966 318
Shortfield Common
. . . . . . . . . . . . . . . . . .3A **40**  SU 842 422
Shortland Copse . . . . .2D **67**  SU 996 321
Shottermill . . . . . . . . . .2E **63**  SU 885 327
Shufflesheeps . . . . . . .5A **62**  SU 845 296
Sidlow . . . . . . . . . . . . .4F **39**  TQ 258 469
Sidlow Bridge  . . . . . . .3F **39**  TQ 258 470
Sidney Wood . . . . . . . .5F **57**  TQ 019 343
Sidney Wood Car Park
. . . . . . . . . . . . . . . . . .4A **58**  TQ 026 351
Silent Pool . . . . . . . . . .2E **33**  TQ 060 485
Silent Pool Car Park . . .2D **33**  TQ 059 484
Silkmill Pond  . . . . . . . .5B **42**  SU 916 406
Single Street . . . . . . . . .2F **11**  TQ 436 598
Six Brothers Field . . . . .2F **21**  TQ 313 547
Slaughter Bridge . . . . . .6F **61**  TQ 134 334
Smithwood Common
. . . . . . . . . . . . . . . . . .4D **47**  TQ 051 414
Snarham Land . . . . . . .4C **56**  SU 981 357
Somersbury Wood . . . .2C **60**  TQ 106 376
Somerset Bridge . . . . . .2C **42**  SU 921 439
South Holmwood . . . . .6D **37**  TQ 171 449
South Merstham . . . . . .4D **21**  TQ 291 524
South Park . . . . . . . . . .2F **39**  TQ 250 488
South Street . . . . . . . . .4F **11**  TQ 431 577
Sparkes Copse . . . . . . .6A **56**  SU 960 337
Sparrwood Hangar . . . .4D **67**  SU 998 302
Spitfire Centre Car Park
. . . . . . . . . . . . . . . . . .2E **11**  TQ 421 590
Spreakley . . . . . . . . . . .4A **40**  SU 839 418
Spynes Mere Nature Reserve
. . . . . . . . . . . . . . . . . .4E **21**  TQ 306 524
Squerryes . . . . . . . . . . .3F **25**  TQ 441 533
Squire's Great Wood
. . . . . . . . . . . . . . . . . .5A **36**  TQ 148 459
Squirrels' Hill . . . . . . . .2C **44**  SU 983 432
Standages . . . . . . . . . .2D **57**  SU 994 374
Standing Wood . . . . . .4D **57**  SU 996 356
Stanley Common . . . . .4B **62**  SU 858 302
Staplelane Copse  . . . . .1F **33**  TQ 070 496

Starrock Wood . . . . . . .4C **6**  TQ 284 574
Steer's Common . . . . . .6E **67**  TQ 006 281
Stock Bridge . . . . . . . .2E **41**  SU 880 430
Stockbridge Car Park
. . . . . . . . . . . . . . . . . .3D **41**  SU 874 429
Stockbridge Pond . . . . .3D **41**  SU 875 422
Stone Bridge  . . . . . . . .4D **31**  SU 999 462
Stonebridge . . . . . . . . .3D **37**  TQ 177 476
Stony Rock Car Park
. . . . . . . . . . . . . . . . . .6E **15**  TQ 124 504
Strood Green . . . . . . . .2A **38**  TQ 200 481
Stroud Common . . . . . .3C **46**  TQ 041 425
Stroud Wood . . . . . . . .4C **54**  SU 922 352
Stubbs Copse . . . . . . . .2E **23**  TQ 367 542
Sussex Border Path . . . .5F **59**  TQ 079 344
. . . . . . . . . . . . . . . . . .4D **61**  TQ 114 354
. . . . . . . . . . . . . . . . . .3D **63**  SU 872 311
. . . . . . . . . . . . . . . . . .4B **64**  SU 915 303
. . . . . . . . . . . . . . . . . .2F **65**  SU 958 328
. . . . . . . . . . . . . . . . . .2E **67**  TQ 007 327
Sutton Abinger . . . . . . .5C **34**  TQ 105 459

Tandridge . . . . . . . . . .6F **23**  TQ 372 507
Tandridge Hill . . . . . . . .3E **23**  TQ 369 535
Tankersford Common
. . . . . . . . . . . . . . . . . .3B **40**  SU 859 427
Tanland Copse . . . . . . .6E **65**  SU 944 285
Tanner's Hatch Youth Hostel
. . . . . . . . . . . . . . . . . .5A **16**  TQ 140 515
The Tarn . . . . . . . . . . .5A **28**  SU 909 457
Tatsfield . . . . . . . . . . . .5D **11**  TQ 412 568
Temple Wood . . . . . . . .6F **51**  TQ 190 391
Tenningshook Wood
. . . . . . . . . . . . . . . . . .5B **34**  TQ 097 451
Thorncombe Street . . . .3D **45**  SU 999 421
Thornet Wood . . . . . . .2D **15**  TQ 115 546
Thundry Meadows Nature Reserve
. . . . . . . . . . . . . . . . . .2F **41**  SU 897 437
Thursley . . . . . . . . . . . .6A **42**  SU 901 397
Thursley Common . . . . .5A **42**  SU 904 409
Thursley Lake . . . . . . . .6C **42**  SU 921 395
Thursley National Nature Reserve
. . . . . . . . . . . . . . . . . .5A **42**  SU 904 401
Thursley National Nature Reserve
  (Elstead Moat) Car Park
. . . . . . . . . . . . . . . . . .4F **41**  SU 899 415
Tidy's Copse . . . . . . . . .1E **67**  TQ 001 334
Tilburstow Hill . . . . . . .6D **23**  TQ 351 501
Tilburstow Hill Car Park
. . . . . . . . . . . . . . . . . .6C **22**  TQ 349 500
Tilburstowhill Common
. . . . . . . . . . . . . . . . . .6D **23**  TQ 355 503
Tilford . . . . . . . . . . . . .2D **41**  SU 874 435
Tilford Common . . . . . .3C **40**  SU 868 423
Tilford Green Car Park
. . . . . . . . . . . . . . . . . .2D **41**  SU 873 434
Tilfordmill Bridge . . . . .1C **40**  SU 868 444
Titsey . . . . . . . . . . . . . .2C **24**  TQ 408 549
Titsey Park . . . . . . . . . .2C **24**  TQ 404 548
Titsey Place . . . . . . . . .1C **24**  TQ 406 550
Titsey Wood . . . . . . . . .2D **25**  TQ 419 542
Tongham . . . . . . . . . . .2E **27**  SU 886 489
Top of Horseblock Hollow
  (Hurtwood 4) Car Park
. . . . . . . . . . . . . . . . . .3F **47**  TQ 074 425
Tower Hill . . . . . . . . . . .2C **36**  TQ 169 482
Townhouse Copse . . . . .6E **61**  TQ 124 334
Tuder's Copse . . . . . . .4B **54**  SU 911 350
Tuesley . . . . . . . . . . . .4A **44**  SU 963 419
Tugley Wood . . . . . . . .1C **66**  SU 980 334
Tunnel Car Park
  (Great Bookham Common)
. . . . . . . . . . . . . . . . . .1E **15**  TQ 129 556
Turnour's Wood . . . . . .3F **65**  SU 959 316
Tyler's Green . . . . . . . .4D **23**  TQ 350 524
Tyndalls Wood . . . . . . .4E **53**  SU 888 354
Tyrell's Wood . . . . . . . .1E **17**  TQ 187 554

Unstead Wood . . . . . . .1D **45**  SU 994 443
Updown Wood . . . . . . .2B **16**  TQ 158 541
Upper Barn Hanger . . .6D **65**  SU 939 284
Upper Canfold Wood
. . . . . . . . . . . . . . . . . .6A **48**  TQ 081 397
Upper Eashing . . . . . . .2F **43**  SU 952 438
Upper Gatton Wood . . .2B **20**  TQ 273 545

Upper Hale . . . . . . . . . .2A **26** SU 841 489
Upper Ifold Wood . . . . .2E **67** TQ 004 328
Upper Warlingham Station
. . . . . . . . . . . . . . . . .3C **8** TQ 340 583

Vachery Pond . . . . . . .2F **59** TQ 070 373
Valewood Park . . . . . .4A **64** SU 905 308
Van Common . . . . . . .5F **63** SU 894 292
Vanguard Way . . . . . . .1E **9** TQ 368 605
. . . . . . . . . . . . . . . . .1A **24** TQ 385 551
. . . . . . . . . . . . . . . . .2C **24** TQ 406 543
. . . . . . . . . . . . . . . . .6F **25** TQ 431 507
Vanhurst Copse . . . . . .1E **53** SU 889 380
Vann Copse . . . . . . . . .2B **56** SU 979 372
Vann Lake . . . . . . . . . .6B **50** TQ 156 395
Velhurst Copse . . . . . . .5A **58** TQ 023 344
Viner's Bridge . . . . . . .3A **40** SU 840 421

Waggoners Wells . . . . .5C **52** SU 860 343
Waggoners Wells Car Park
. . . . . . . . . . . . . . . . .5C **52** SU 862 344
Walk Copse . . . . . . . .2A **66** SU 964 323
Walking Bottom, Peaslake
(Hurtwood 2) Car Park
. . . . . . . . . . . . . . . . .1A **48** TQ 083 444
Walliswood . . . . . . . . .1D **61** TQ 118 381
Wallis Wood Nature Reserve
. . . . . . . . . . . . . . . . .1E **61** TQ 123 388
Walton Heath . . . . . . .3C **18** TQ 229 537
Walton Heath Car Park
. . . . . . . . . . . . . . . . .2C **18** TQ 227 544
Walton on the Hill . . . .1C **18** TQ 222 550
Walton Park Wood . . . .2B **18** TQ 216 544
Wanborough . . . . . . . .2D **29** SU 933 489
Wanborough Common
. . . . . . . . . . . . . . . . .3E **29** SU 945 474
Wanborough Wood . . .1C **28** SU 922 490
Wardley Hanger . . . . . .6A **62** SU 844 289
Warlingham . . . . . . . . .3D **9** TQ 356 585
Warren Hill . . . . . . . . .1C **42** SU 925 443
Warren Pond . . . . . . . .4A **28** SU 908 460
Waterloo Pond . . . . . . .2C **32** TQ 042 480
Watts Chapel . . . . . . . .3F **29** SU 956 473
Watts Gallery . . . . . . . .3F **29** SU 958 478
Watts Hill . . . . . . . . . .4E **25** TQ 421 529
Waverley Abbey . . . . . .5C **26** SU 867 452

Waverley Abbey Car Park
. . . . . . . . . . . . . . . . .5D **27** SU 870 455
Waverleymill Bridge . . .5D **27** SU 870 455
Weald Barkfold Copse
. . . . . . . . . . . . . . . . .2E **67** TQ 003 325
West Clandon . . . . . . .4C **12** TQ 044 524
Westcott . . . . . . . . . . .2A **36** TQ 141 486
Westcott Heath . . . . . .2F **35** TQ 136 483
Westerham Wood . . . . .2F **25** TQ 438 549
West Hanger Car Park
. . . . . . . . . . . . . . . . .1F **33** TQ 070 493
West Horsley . . . . . . . .4F **13** TQ 078 523
Westhumble . . . . . . . . .5C **16** TQ 163 518
Westhumble Chapel
. . . . . . . . . . . . . . . . .5B **16** TQ 159 519
West Kent Golf Course Nature Reserve
. . . . . . . . . . . . . . . . .1E **11** TQ 428 608
Westwood Common
. . . . . . . . . . . . . . . . .4A **38** TQ 202 462
Wet Wood . . . . . . . . . .6A **66** SU 962 287
Wey and Arun Canal
. . . . . . . . . . . . . . . . .2B **58** TQ 039 373
Weybourne . . . . . . . . .2B **26** SU 854 488
Weydown Common . . .5A **54** SU 902 343
Wey-South Path . . . . . .2D **31** SU 994 486
. . . . . . . . . . . . . . . . .2F **45** TQ 017 436
. . . . . . . . . . . . . . . . .5B **46** TQ 038 404
. . . . . . . . . . . . . . . . .6F **57** TQ 018 338
Wheelerstreet . . . . . . . .5E **43** SU 946 406
Whiteberry Gate . . . . . .1F **49** TQ 139 441
White Down Car Park
. . . . . . . . . . . . . . . . .1D **35** TQ 114 494
White Downs . . . . . . . .1D **35** TQ 119 494
Whitefield Hanger . . . . .2E **55** SU 945 371
White Hill . . . . . . . . . .3E **17** TQ 182 534
. . . . . . . . . . . . . . . . .3A **22** TQ 322 538
Whitehill Car Park . . . .4D **17** TQ 176 529
White Post . . . . . . . . . .6B **22** TQ 334 505
Whitmoor Vale . . . . . . .3C **52** SU 861 363
Whyteleafe . . . . . . . . . .3B **8** TQ 334 585
Whyteleafe South Station
. . . . . . . . . . . . . . . . .4C **8** TQ 341 577
Whyteleafe Station . . . .3B **8** TQ 338 585
Wildfield Copse . . . . . .1F **29** SU 953 499
Wildwood Copse . . . . .4D **59** TQ 053 353
Willinghurst Lake . . . . .3D **47** TQ 050 421
Winders Hill . . . . . . . . .3D **23** TQ 354 538
Windfall Wood . . . . . . .6C **64** SU 925 282

Windfallwood Common
. . . . . . . . . . . . . . . . .6C **64** SU 927 279
Winkworth Arboretum
. . . . . . . . . . . . . . . . .4D **45** SU 993 412
Winterfold ("Donkins")
(Hurtwood 5) Car Park
. . . . . . . . . . . . . . . . .3E **47** TQ 063 426
Winterfold Heath . . . . .3E **47** TQ 061 429
Winterfold (Northside)
(Hurtwood 13) Car Park
. . . . . . . . . . . . . . . . .3F **47** TQ 073 425
Winterfold ("Radar Site")
(Hurtwood 6) Car Park
. . . . . . . . . . . . . . . . .3D **47** TQ 058 426
Winterfold Wood . . . . .2E **47** TQ 068 435
Witley . . . . . . . . . . . . .6E **43** SU 947 398
Witley Common . . . . . .5C **42** SU 929 408
Witley Common Car Park
. . . . . . . . . . . . . . . . .5D **43** SU 932 406
Witley Common Nature Centre
. . . . . . . . . . . . . . . . .5D **43** SU 932 405
Witley Park . . . . . . . . .6C **42** SU 924 391
Witley Station . . . . . . .2E **55** SU 948 379
Woldingham . . . . . . . . .6F **9** TQ 370 558
Woldingham Garden Village
. . . . . . . . . . . . . . . . .4E **9** TQ 363 570
Woldingham Station . . .5D **9** TQ 359 563
Wonersh . . . . . . . . . . .5F **31** TQ 016 462
Wonersh Common . . . .4F **31** TQ 017 463
Woodhatch . . . . . . . . .2F **39** TQ 258 488
Woodhill . . . . . . . . . . .2C **46** TQ 041 435
Woodmansterne . . . . . .2B **6** TQ 276 599
Woodmansterne Station
. . . . . . . . . . . . . . . . .2C **6** TQ 287 593
Woolmer Hill . . . . . . . .1D **63** SU 877 330
Wormley . . . . . . . . . . .1E **55** SU 949 382
Worms Heath . . . . . . . .4F **9** TQ 378 578
Wotton . . . . . . . . . . . .3E **35** TQ 126 476
Wotton Common . . . . .1F **49** TQ 134 440
Wray Common . . . . . . .6A **20** TQ 267 509
Wray Lane Car Park . . .4A **20** TQ 262 523

Yagden Hill . . . . . . . . .3E **41** SU 886 423
Yewen's Hanger . . . . . .3F **55** SU 951 365

Zig Zag Car Park . . . . .5D **17** TQ 176 519

# Safety & Security when walking

## GENERAL

◆ Make sure you are wearing appropriate clothing and footwear, with suitable extra clothing in case the weather changes, or if you get delayed or misjudge how long it will take you to complete the walk.
◆ Be careful, if you are inexperienced, not to undertake a walk that is too ambitious.
◆ Take plenty to eat and drink, there are not always opportunities to buy extra
◆ provisions.
   Be sure someone knows where you are going and when to expect you back. Let them know when you have returned as well.
◆ Although taking a mobile phone is a good idea, in some remote areas there may not be a signal and therefore should not be relied upon.
◆ When walking on roads follow the advice in the Highway Code.
◆ Always use a pavement and safe crossing points whenever possible.
◆ Where there is no pavement it is better to walk on the right hand side of the road, facing oncoming traffic.
◆ Only cross railway lines at designated places and never walk along railway lines.
◆ Good navigational skills and a compass are essential.
◆ Always take warm and waterproof clothing; conditions at coastal locations can always change quickly, even in summer.
◆ Walking boots should always be worn.
◆ Gloves and headgear are advisable too in cold weather.
◆ Other essentials to take are; a waterproof backpack, "high energy" foods, a whistle, a torch (with spare batteries and bulb), a watch, a first aid kit, water purification tablets and a survival bag.
◆ Ready made first aid kits are available with all necessary items included.
◆ High factor sunscreen should be used in sunny weather, the sun can be particularly strong and can be hidden by sea breezes. Sunglasses are advisable too.
◆ Informal paths leading to beaches can be dangerous and are best avoided.
◆ When crossing a beach, make sure you know the tide times to avoid being cut off.
◆ Some cliffs overhang or are unstable and this are not always obvious.
◆ On the coast, mist, fog and high winds are more likely and can be hazardous.

The international distress signal is six blasts of a whistle repeated at one minute intervals (the reply is three) or six flashes of light at one minute intervals (again the reply is three). In an emergency dial 999, or 112 and ask for the coastguard.

MOD - Defence Training Estate
This Ministry of Defense land is held solely for the purpose of training the Armed Forces.

For Managed Access land obey all signs and bylaws relevant to the area being visited.

DTE South East (including Home Counties)

MANAGED ACCESS - Page 26. Aldershot and Minley training areas.
The majority of the area is designated as a Site of Special Scientific Interest.

For further information on access please contact the Defence Training Estate Training Area Officer on 01483 798357.

MANAGED ACCESS - Page 52. Bramshott Common.

MANAGED ACCESS - Page 42. Elstead Common.

MANAGED ACCESS - Page 41. Hankley Common.

The Commons represent some of the finest remaining heathland in Southern England and are nationally important for their bird, reptile and invertebrate populations.

For further information on access to the Commons telephone 01420 483375.

## THE COUNTRYSIDE CODE

◆ Be safe - plan ahead and follow any signs.
Even when going out locally, it's best to get the latest information about where and when you can go; for example, your rights to go onto some areas of open land may be restricted while work is carried out, for safety reasons or during breeding seasons. Follow advice and local signs, and be prepared for the unexpected.
◆ Leave gates and property as you find them.
Please respect the working life of the countryside, as our actions can affect people's livelihoods, our heritage, and the safety and welfare of animals and ourselves.
◆ Protect plants and animals, and take your litter home.
We have a responsibility to protect our countryside now and for future generations, so make sure you don't harm animals, birds, plants, or trees. Fires can be as devastating to wildlife and habitats as they are to people and property.
◆ Keep dogs under close control.
The countryside is a great place to exercise dogs, but it's every owner's duty to make sure their dog is not a danger or nuisance to farm animals, wildlife or other people.
◆ Consider other people.
Showing consideration and respect for other people makes the countryside a pleasant environment for everyone - at home, at work and at leisure.

Vineyard at Dorking

# Mountain Biking

## Technical and Safety Tips

### Take care

Always wear a helmet, it may save your life! Ride within your capabilities and skills and allow plenty of time for your ride. Before leaving ensure your bike is safe by checking tyres, brakes and gears. Tell someone where you are going and what time you intend to return. Take the appropriate map, compass, basic first aid kit, food, money and mobile phone.

### Tools

Always carry a basic tool kit; a cycling specific multi-tool is best, but if not you will need 4mm, 5mm and 6mm allen keys, small flat head and Phillips screwdriver. Also make sure you carry a pump, tyre levers, puncture repair kit and some spare inner tubes. It is easier to replace a tube than to fix a puncture.

### Clothing

Make sure you are prepared for all weather conditions by wearing several layers of clothing that can be adjusted. Take a lightweight waterproof jacket, even in fine weather. Padded cycling shorts are a must and can be worn under leggings in cold condition.

## Code of Conduct

◆ Give way to horse riders and pedestrians, slow down, say "Hello" and give way.

◆ Don't disturb wildlife, plants or trees.

◆ Keep to published routes.

◆ Always leave gates as you find them.

◆ Take rubbish away with you.

◆ Don't light fires.

◆ Keep away from forestry operations.

◆ Expect the unexpected.

◆ Avoid back wheel skids, which can cause erosion.

◆ At all times, please be considerate and courteous to those you meet on route.

◆ Slow down when approaching and travelling through farmyards and respect our local farmers when crossing their land.